ROMAN ORTHOËPY:

A PLEA

FOR THE RESTORATION

OF THE

TRUE SYSTEM

OF

LATIN PRONUNCIATION.

BY

JOHN F. RICHARDSON,

PROFESSOR OF THE LATIN LANGUAGE AND LITERATURE IN THE UNIVERSITY OF ROCHESTER.

NEW YORK:

SHELDON & COMPANY,

115 NASSAU STREET.

1859.

ELECTROTYPED BY
THOMAS B. SMITH & SON
82 & 84 Beekman-street.

PRINTED BY
PUDNEY & RUSSELL,
79 John-street.

PREFACE.

The author of this little Manual was, from 1838 to 1850, professor of the Latin language and literature in Madison University. During the latter part of that period, he became dissatisfied with the English mode of pronouncing Latin, and convinced that a change, at least so far as to substitute the German for the English vowel sounds, would be, intrinsically, a great improvement. But the fancied inconveniences of a change—inconveniences which experience has taught him were greatly exaggerated—together with a strong repugnance to the notoriety of singularity, presented obstacles which his conviction of its inherent advantages was then unable to surmount.

Immediately after the organization of this University, in the autumn of 1850, his attention was again called to this question, and he was induced to institute a new and still more careful examination of the whole subject of Latin pronunciation. The result of that examination was a thorough conviction, not only of the possibility, but of the decided expediency, of restoring the Roman method of pronouncing the language. He submitted to the Faculty of the University the most important considerations which had led him to that conclusion, and obtained their approval and sanction of the proposed change. But again his courage was unequal to a total reform. By way of compromise, and as a tentative, he adopted the Roman sounds of the vowels and diphthongs, and of the consonants J, S, and T, but shrank from the greatest and, perhaps, the most important change to the Roman sounds of C, G, and QV. Where the English sounds of these letters differed from the Roman, he was in the habit of suggesting to his higher classes, for the purpose of explaining some point in etymology, prosody or comparative philology, &c., the Roman pronunciation of the word in question; and the almost invariable response which he received from his pupils was the inquiry, "Why then do you not pronounce it so?" This question it was easy to evade but not to answer satisfactorily, either to his more intelligent pupils or to himself.

In the latter part of 1851, there appeared in the New York Recorder, a review of Professor Haldeman's able treatise on "Latin Pronunciation," from the pen of the late lamented Robert Kelly, LL. D., of that city, one of the founders and most influential managers of this University, and a man of the highest style of classical scholarship, earnestly and ably advocating the general adoption, in our literary institutions, of the Roman method of pronouncing Latin. Delighted with the suggestions of this reviewer, which were in such full accordance with my own convictions, and greatly strengthened in the soundness of those conclusions by his cogent reasonings and illustrations, I determined to introduce the true system *entire* to my own classes without waiting any longer for the coöperation of other institutions. In this position the author has had no occasion for self-condemnation. He has met, as he expected, with some opposition and a little reproach; but he has been more than satisfied with the working of his system, and he has been sustained and cheered by the cordial sympathy and coöperation of his pupils.

The following Manual has been prepared in compliance with the requests of several literary friends and classical teachers in other institutions, who have called on the author for a description of the Roman system, and his reasons for using it.

It is proper to say that, as the work is designed for the use of learners as well as teachers of Latin, the author has, in many cases, made the arguments and illustrations more full than he would have deemed necessary or appropriate had he been writing exclusively for the latter class of readers

In the preparation of the Manual, the author would acknowledge his indebtedness to the work of Charles Kraitsir, M.D., entitled "Glossology," published in 1852, for some important facts and proofs in relation to the early English-Latin pronunciation, and for several of the extracts from the Latin grammarians which are found in the appendix of this work.

With these explanations, the Manual is now submitted to the public, in the hope that it may contribute to the general abandonment of the diverse, conflicting, unscientific and unscholarly methods now in use, and the substitution of that one which is demonstrably correct and alone correct.

ROMAN ORTHOËPY.

It is a very common opinion that there are but two widely prevalent systems of Latin pronunciation, the English and the Continental, and that these differ only in the sounds they respectively assign to the vowels. A large majority of the modern Latin grammars and elementary works published in our language for the use of English and American students, have given expression to this opinion, and many of them have laid down rules for the sounds of the vowels in each of the two systems; and then, assuming that there is but one common mode of sounding the consonants and diphthongs, they simply offer the student his choice between these two vowel systems as his only alternative in respect of Latin pronunciation. They either give him or leave him to understand that, according as he connects with these common sounds the one or the other of the two vowel systems, he will have either the English or the Continental system, pure and entire.

Now what are the facts in respect to the different modes of pronouncing Latin? In the first place, there are two distinct and very different English systems of Latin pronunciation, the earlier and the later. In the second place, it is an entire misnomer to speak of the "Continental Method" of pronouncing Latin. There is, in fact, no common Continental system, but there are several Continental systems of Latin pronunciation, *e. g.*, German, Italian, French, Spanish. These four agree, to be sure, substantially in regard to the vowels; but, in other important points, they differ decidedly both from the English and from each other, most of the diphthongs and some of the most important consonants being sounded differently in all five. The idea, therefore, that he who combines the German vowel sounds with the English diphthongal and consonant sounds has *the* Continental system or *any* Continental system of Latin pronunciation, is simply absurd.

Of the *six* different systems of Latin pronunciation, then, prevailing in western Europe and our own country, five are strictly *national.* Their differences find at once an origin and an explanation in the fact that the scholars of each nation have followed, in their pronunciation of the Latin, the analogies of their own vernacular. In this way, while making sure of mutual disagreement, *all* have departed more or less from the true Roman method, and the whole subject has been involved in uncertainty and confusion. Meanwhile the pseudo-Continental system, destitute alike of historical dignity and scientific accuracy, and lacking even the poor support of national prejudice and pride, is powerless to mediate and compose these differences. Although it undoubtedly avoids some of the grossest absurdities peculiar to the English system, it lacks the elements which command respect, and can never establish a claim to universal adoption and use.

Under these circumstances, it is not strange that the expediency of attempting a restoration of the Roman pronunciation should, for many years, have engaged the attention of prominent Latin scholars in all countries. So numerous, so constant, and so serious are the practical evils connected with the want of a uniform standard, and still more, with the *falsity* of the methods in actual use, that the question of restoring the true pronunciation is continually forcing itself upon the mind of the earnest

Latinist as one of vital importance to the dignity, the value and the progress of Latin philology.*

These evils manifest themselves most fully where

* Justus Lipsius, in his "DIALOGUS DE RECTA PRONUNCIATIONE LINGUAE LATINAE," expresses himself upon the false pronunciation of the consonant *c*, in this forcible and felicitous manner:—"PUDET NON TAM ERRORIS QVAM PERTINACIAE, QVIA CORRIPI PATIUNTUR AT NON CORRIGI, ET TENENT OMNES QVOD DEFENDAT NEMO. ITALI, HISPANI, GERMANI, GALLI, BRITANNI, IN HOC PECCATO; A QVA GENTE INITIUM EMENDANDI? AUDEAT ENIM UNA ALIQVA ET OMNES AUDIENT."

The Rt. Hon. W. E. Gladstone, D.C.L., M. P. for the University of Oxford, at the close of the Prolegomena to Homer and the Homeric Age, employs the following language:

"Finally, though sharing the dissatisfaction of others at the established preference given among us to the Latin names of deities originally Greek, and at some part of our orthography for Greek names, I have thought it best to adhere in general to the common custom and only to deviate from it where a special object was in view. I fear that diversity and even confusion are more likely to arise, than any benefit, from efforts at reform made by individuals, and without the advantage either of authority or of a clear principle, as a groundwork for general consent. I am here disposed to say, '*οὐκ ἀγαθὸν πολυκοιρανίη*;' and again with Wordsworth,

"'Me this unchartered freedom tires;'

yet I should gladly see the day when, under the authority of scholars, and especially of those who bear rule in places of education, improvement might be effected not only in the points above mentioned, but in our solitary and barbarous method of pronouncing both the Greek and the Latin language. In this one respect the European world may still with justice describe the English at least as the 'PENITUS TOTO DIVISOS ORBE BRITANNOS.'"

the present English system of Latin pronunciation obtains—a system which deviates most widely from the Roman, and is most decidedly at war with the structure and genius of the Latin language; and here especially, the restoration of the vernacular pronunciation becomes a matter of urgent practical moment.

I have spoken of the present English system of Latin pronunciation in distinction from an earlier and much purer method which formerly prevailed in England, and which accorded substantially with the Roman. Although the English is now the most irregular and confused of all the alphabets of Europe, yet no modern tongue entered upon its career as a written language, with better prospects of securing a harmonious system of orthoëpy than the Anglo-Saxon. To this language the Roman alphabet was very skillfully adapted. All the sounds which the two languages had in common were represented by characters taken from the Roman alphabet, while those which were wanting in the Latin were indicated by characters newly invented, or borrowed from other alphabets. C and G, *e. g.*, which are now so frequently employed respectively as *lingual* and *dental spirants* (the former having the sound of S sharp, and the latter, that of J, a sound unknown alike to the Anglo-Saxon and the Latin), were in all Saxon, as well as in all Latin words, employed as *guttural mutes*, representing the hard and soft K-sounds. The unequaled irregularities of English orthoëpy are attributable, not to the lack of sagacity and good judgment on the part of our Anglo-Saxon ancestors, but to the undue influence of the Norman conquerors of England over its language as well as over its laws and customs. But a substantially correct Latin pronunciation had been established in England long before the Norman conquest; and while, after that event, the higher classes in that country, in the spirit of undiscriminating subserviency to the superior civilization and refinement of their conquerors, imitated alike, and with equal readiness, their errors and their virtues, and thus sacrificed some of the best peculiarities of their own language to the irregularities of the French, this pure Latin pronunciation maintained its ground until a comparatively recent period. Not until about the middle of the last century was the process of its corruption fully completed. Nor, meanwhile, did it escape the sharp censure and earnest protests of many noble English scholars, who attempted, at different periods, either to arrest the progress of this corruption, or to reform the pronunciation when corrupted. The Latin grammars formerly used in England contain many cautions against falling into the vulgar errors. One of these, first published in the reign of Henry the Eighth, lays the following injunction upon the Latin teacher :—

"ANTE OMNIA DETERRENDI SUNT PUERI AB IIS VITIIS QVAE NOSTRO VULGO PAENE PROPRIA ESSE VIDENTUR."

At this period of English history very great attention was paid to the study of the Latin. The elementary works employed in the schools abound in warnings, not only against grave errors of pronunciation, but also against minor faults of articulation. The teacher is urged to see to it that the pupil shall not merely preserve the pure sounds of the letters but that he shall utter those sounds ORE ROTUNDO. Philology, it is true, was not then understood or cultivated as a science, and no special value was set on the *scientific* importance of preserving the sounds of the language unchanged ; but the superiority of euphony to cacophony, of harmony to discord, was fully appreciated, and thus on principles of good taste, though not of philological science, the scholars of that and of the two succeeding centuries sought to preserve unimpaired the purity and beauty of Latin orthoëpy. The most distinguished men of those times took a lively interest in the preservation of this system. In a letter addressed by Cardinal Wolsey to the masters of his school at Ipswich, he exhorts the teachers to use great diligence in forming the tender lips of their pupils to an elegant and correct Latin pronunciation:

"QVORUM* OS TENERUM FORMARE PRAECIPUA CURA VOBIS SIT, UTPOTE QVI ET APERTISSIMA ET ELEGANTISSIMA VOCIS PRONUNCIATIONE, TRADITA ELEMENTA PROFERANT."

In like manner, the learned men of the seventeenth and eighteenth centuries endeavored to maintain the pure sounds of the language, and remonstrated against the growing corruption of Latin pronunciation, urging, among other considerations, that unless this process of deterioration was arrested, the language would no longer serve as a medium of oral communication between English

* Since, in the classical period of the Latin language, the character V employed uniformly after Q, became in that position, entirely silent, and was thus merely a part of a compound character representing a single consonant sound, viz., that of K, and the modern rounded character U, if introduced at all into Latin, should be employed only for the V VOCALIS of the Romans, I have thought it proper invariably to retain the V after Q.

and Continental scholars. Prominent among those who thus censured the increasing barbarity of the English mode of pronouncing Latin, stands the majestic and classical Milton. In the letter which he addressed to Mr. Hartlib on the subject of education he lays down among the first rules for the exercises of the pupils in his model school the following direction in respect to their instruction in Latin:

"Their speech is to be fashioned to a distinct and clear pronunciation, as near as possible to the *Italian*, especially in vowels. For we Englishmen, being far northerly, do not open our mouths in the cold air wide enough to grace a southern tongue, but are observed by all other nations to speak exceeding close and inward; so that *to smatter Latin with an English tongue, is as ill a hearing as Law-French.*"

The closeness of which he here complains in the English method of pronouncing Latin, was most apparent, undoubtedly, in the sound of the vowels to which he expressly alludes, and particularly in the sound of the open or back vowels; and it is worthy of notice how fully this precept and remonstrance harmonize with the "APERTISSIMA VOCIS PRONUNCIATIO," recommended by Cardinal Wolsey to the teachers of his own school.

Robert Ainsworth, Thesaur. Ling. Lat., Lond., 1746, in a very valuable preface on Latin pronunciation, which has been improperly, if not dishonestly omitted in the American school editions, says, "With much reluctance, I remark that foreigners hold us little better than barbarians in many parts of pronunciation." He particularly censures the neglect of the quantity of vowels, and the "depraved sound" of c and g before AE, OE, E, I. "The irregular and uncertain pronunciation of these letters proves often a great discouragement to those who desire to learn our tongue; and this, together with our different sounds of the vowels, makes our Latin, though much purer generally (meaning, *in structure*,) than theirs, almost as unintelligible as our English. . . . . This I leave to the consideration and redress of the learned schoolmasters of this kingdom, as well deserving it. . . . To say NASHIO, instead of NATIO, T as in TILL, is absurd, if we did not *submit* to a barbarous prescription."

Philipps, a preceptor to some of the princes of the royal family, a man of superior classical attainments, and very familiar also with many modern tongues, in his "Method of Teaching Languages," published in 1750, complains of the very faulty and unpleasant manner in which Englishmen pronounce

Latin. He describes his mode of teaching this language to a youth placed in his charge, and tells us that he took "special care" to wean him from his awkward manner of pronouncing.

"He gave me a great deal of trouble for some months on this head; so that I had much ado to persuade him to *open* his mouth; for he pronounced the vowels very badly, especially the A and E; for instead of AMO, he pronounced EMO; and when he pronounced EMO, *to buy*, he called it IMO; and instead of IMO, *yes*, he said AIMO." He speaks of this inelegant mode of pronouncing Latin as of a thing common, yet not universal. "Many gentlemen in England," is his pertinent observation, "still speak Latin like men, ORE ROTUNDO."

Dr. Foster (Essay on Accent and Quantity) complains of the "violence done to the quantity of the ancient languages by the English pronunciation, and that, though an attachment be *professed* to it, yet this very quantity they do all (most of them without knowing it,) most grossly corrupt."

Mitford (Inquiry into the Principles of Harmony in Language, published at the close of the eighteenth century,) points out the absurdity of introducing into Latin the *eccentric* pronunciation of the English; he represents its *incompatibility* with the true quantity of syllables, and proposes the restoration of the ancient sounds of the vowels, as in Italian.

But in spite of these warnings, remonstrances, and regrets of prominent English scholars, this corruption of Latin pronunciation went on, and was finally and fully effected about the middle of the last century. Since that time, this method of pronouncing Latin has been reduced to a grave system, and is formally inculcated in nearly all the manuals of Latin instruction prepared in our language for the use of English and American students. No one pretends to claim for it any scientific or historical basis. It is justified solely on grounds of prescription, convenience and *nationality*, and yet it is enforced by precept and example in a very large majority of the literary institutions of this country and of England.

The young student opens his Latin grammar, or comes to his Latin teacher, and is informed, at the outset, that, the Roman system of Latin pronunciation being in a great measure lost, each of the different modern nations follows, in its pronunciation of this language, the analogies of its own. This is all the information that is usually afforded him on the subject. Occasionally, within a few years past, there has appeared some elementary work which has expressed a preference for the so-called "Continental Method," and, that the student may take his choice between the two systems, the author proceeds to give the system of *vowel* sounds supposed to prevail on the Continent, and especially in Germany. But not one of these works, so far as my observation extends, has given the *real* distinction between the long and short sounds of the German vowels; and thus a system of vowel sounds which nowhere exists on the Continent of Europe, is to be combined with the English consonant sounds to form what is called the "Continental Method" of Latin pronunciation, but which can be justly denominated "Continental" only because it has, by these means, obtained a partial foothold on the continent of North America.

This, I think, is a fair statement of the amount of light, if light it may be called, which our English manuals of Latin instruction shed on the subject of Latin pronunciation. Not a hint is given that the English pronunciation of Latin deviates from the Roman far more than that of the other nations of Europe; not an inkling is vouchsafed of the clear and abundant proofs by which the correct sounds of the Roman letters have been established; not a gleam of light is thrown on the intimate and most interesting connection between the *sounds* which enter into and compose a language and its pervading genius, the structure and harmony of its verse and its affinities in the great family of speech. On all these points an absolute silence is maintained. The pupil is informed that, in the absence of any other guide, he is at full liberty to conform his Latin pronunciation to what is termed "English analogy," but, with the exception of those falsely-exhibited Continental vowel sounds, he has no light and no liberty given him to do any thing else; and, as if the more certainly to insure an absolute uniformity in error, this English analogy is expounded in a set of rules which require the constant perversion of the pure sounds and violation of the true quantities of the Latin language.

These charges I hold myself bound to make good before I close the present discussion. The proofs, however, can be more clearly presented and their force will be more readily appreciated after a careful consideration of the true Roman system, to which I now proceed. But, says one, the Latin ceased some twelve or thirteen hundred years since to be a living language, and in these circumstances, can the Roman pronunciation of it be satisfactorily ascertained? Every one who has properly investigated the subject will answer this question in the affirmative. Latin pronunciation with the Romans, was perfectly simple and invariable. The writings of the ancient Latin grammarians contain the most elaborate discussions in respect to the sounds of the letters; every variation even of the vowel sounds is noticed and the exact position of the organs in the enunciation of each letter is described as accurately as the nature of the subject admits. The entire silence of these authors with regard to so remarkable an irregularity in the notation of the Latin language as the use of one character to denote totally distinct sounds, would be, in itself, sufficient proof that no such irregularity existed. In addition to this explicit testimony of those whose statements are authoritative, the incidental proofs found in other writings, and especially in the language itself—in its obvious laws of vowel, diphthongal and consonant changes—are innumerable and entirely harmonious both with each other and with the statements of the Latin grammarians and rhetoricians. Schneider, in his "Elementarlehre der Lateinischen Sprache," gives the results with great minuteness, and with references to fifty ancient authors. The object of this Manual will be accomplished by a succinct statement of those results accompanied, as we advance, by such illustrations and proofs as the limits of our discussion will admit.

The exceeding simplicity and regularity of the Roman system render it, fortunately, an easy thing to exhibit, and of course easy to teach and to learn; and its beautiful consistency and completeness once clearly apprehended, carry with them so much of the force of an internal demonstration as to need comparatively little corroboration from outward and incidental proofs.

A.

SOUNDS OF THE VOWELS.

It is a distinguishing and excellent feature of this system that each alphabetical character, with some few and slight exceptions, represents but one elementary sound.

Each of the vowel letters, however, like the *α*, *ι*, and *υ*, of the Greek system, stands for both the short and the long sound of the vowel. But these sounds, while differing in quantity, do not differ *radically* in quality. Unquestionably a slight modification of the quality of the sound is sometimes made necessary by the change of quantity, but this, in no case, amounts to a radical change. The long and short sounds of each vowel are, in quality, substantially identical.

The vowels (A, E, I, O, U,) are arranged in the alphabet in a natural series, which is determined by the position of the organs in sounding them. There is a certain point in a scale extending from the throat to the lips, where each sound is articulated—A is formed in the throat; E in the back part of the mouth; I near the teeth; O between the teeth and the lips; U in the lips. Again, in uttering the sound A, the lips are opened widest; in E, they approach each other slightly; in I, they approach still nearer, so that they are closed at the corners, and the mouth has now its widest lateral extension; in O, they are rounded; and in U, they are both rounded and protruded. See Appendix, note A.

The following may be given as a scheme of the vowel sounds:—

Ă	sounds like			the	Eng.	ăh,	as in	DĂ-BAM.
Ā	"	"		"	"	āh,	"	NĀ-BAM.
Ĕ	"	" a	in	"	"	făte,	"	VĔ-NI-O.
Ē	"	" a	"	"	"	fāne,	"	VĒ-NI.
Ĭ	"	" ee	"	"	"	fle͜et,	"	VĬ-DE-O.

ī sounds like	ee	in	the	Eng.	flee̅	"	VĪ-DI.
ŏ "	" o	"	"	"	nŏte,	"	FŎ-VE-O.
ō "	" o	"	"	"	tōne,	"	FŌ-VI.
ŭ "	" oo	"	"	"	bo͝ot,	"	FŬ-GI-O.
ū "	" oo	"	"	"	mo͞on,	"	FŪ-GI.

Y, used only in Greek derivatives, sounds nearly like the French *u*.

We would here request the reader to keep in mind an important difference between the Roman and the English principle of syllabication. On the Roman system, a single consonant standing between two vowels, belongs to the latter; and any two or more consonants, which may together begin a word, belong, when standing between two vowels, to the latter vowel. Hence the syllables of NŌBILIS are not NŎB-I-LIS, but NŌ-BI-LIS; of COGNOSCO, not *cog-nos-co*, but *co-gno-sco*, because we have, *e. g.*, such words as GNA-RUS and SCI-PI-O. These rules, however, do not apply to the case of compound words, where the syllabication is determined by the component parts, *e. g.*, the syllables of INTERERAM, are not IN-TE-RE-RAM, but IN-TER-E-RAM.

B.

SOUNDS OF THE DIPHTHONGS.

As each of the five Roman vowel letters represents but one radical sound, varying only in quantity, so, in conformity with this strict and beautiful simplicity of the vowel system, the sound of each of the two elements composing the Latin diphthong was distinctly heard, and each diphthong preserved uniformly the same sound. The only difference, *e. g.*, between AI as a diphthong and as a dissyllable, was, that in the former the two sounds were uttered with one emission of the breath through the voice-passage, and in the latter, with two such emissions.

Of the above Latin vowels, A is the most full and open; next to A, in fullness and openness, come E and O; I and U are closer articulations, allied respectively to E and O, and are either semi-vowels, or, passing from the vowel to the consonant sound, are semi-consonants. Now in every diphthong, whatever be the initial sound, the lips seem most naturally either to be extended laterally so as to be closed at the corners and drawn near to each other at the centre, or to be protruded and rounded, until the I or U sound respectively is reached as the vanish of the diphthong, and in accordance with this natural tendency of the human voice in combining vowel sounds, the Latin diphthong consists properly of an open vowel followed by a semi-vowel, as follows, viz.:

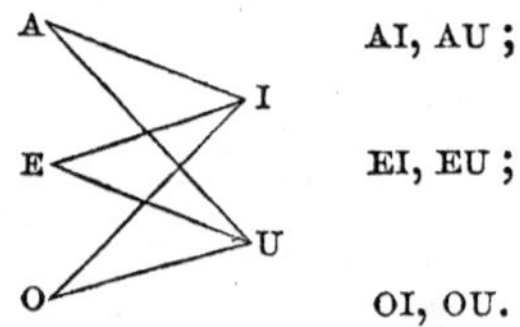

AI, AU;

EI, EU;

OI, OU.

These were *in fact* the *original* diphthongs, the exact counterpart of which is seen in the Greek system, where the A, E, and O-sounds are each followed by *iota* and *upsilon*.

Of these, however, the EI and EU are obviously difficult combinations. The E, being articulated near the middle of the voice-passage, and being also a weaker sound than A or O, is not easily, and therefore not naturally, employed as the initial sound of a diphthong, on which sound, of course, the principal stress of the voice will generally rest, and which, therefore, needs to be a strong vowel. Accordingly, we find that those combinations, though occurring not unfrequently in earlier times, were gradually changed into simple vowels, until the former remained only in the two interjections HEI, EIA, and also in DEIN when contracted into one syllable, as is usual in poetry; and the latter, only in HEUS, HEU, EHEU, CEU, SEU, NEU, NEUTER, and NEUTIQVAM. Even in these hard combinations the Romans adhered firmly to the principle of sound ing distinctly the two elements of the diphthong, so that the word NEUTER, *e. g.*, was by some regarded as properly a trissyllable, although the poets use it as a dissyllable. With the above few exceptions, we have, then, simply the two strongest vowels A and O followed by the two semi-vowels, I and U, thus:—

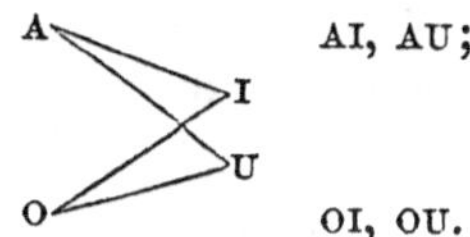

AI, AU;

OI, OU.

These were the *most common* original diphthongs.

But subsequently, as the Latin grammarians state, and the monuments of the language clearly show, the AI and OI came to be written usually AE and OE, the sound remaining essentially unchanged. This change of character must be regarded as a mere orthographic corruption, growing out of the close resemblance between these two vowel sounds;

a resemblance which might easily pass for identity in the vanish of a diphthong as we know that it did sometimes in a short unaccented syllable. Cf. CAERĔMONIA and CAERĬMONIA, INTELLĔGO and INTELLĬGO. Indeed, as a simple matter of fact, no orthographic change occurs more frequently in the early monuments of language than that between E and O, I and U respectively. But though the character E was substituted for I, yet the *voice* would not naturally stop with or vanish on the more open E sound, but would advance to the closely allied and more slender sound which is articulated with the extreme lateral extension of the lips. It was a natural result, then, that when E took the *place*, it also took the *sound* of I after A and O. In the early period of the language, for example, we find such forms as AIDILIS, QVAISTOR, QVAIRERE, etc., instead of AEDILIS, QVAESTOR, QVAERERE, etc. It is contrary to all analogy and all probability to suppose that the popular pronunciation of such words was changed with the written character. Again, we find that the Romans expressed the Greek *AI* and *OI* by AE and OE. And to make the demonstration perfect, the ancient grammarians agree in the statement that the AE and OE took the *sound* as well as the *place* of AI and OI. See Appendix, note B.

The diphthong OU is found only in the early language. In consequence, no doubt, of the slight difference between the O and U sounds, the diphthong was supplanted by U, which of course, was regularly long. Thus the ancient JOUS, JOUSTUS, JOUSTITIA, became JŪS, JŪSTUS, JŪSTITIA. So JOUBEO, JOUBERE, JOUSSI, JOUSSUM, became JUBEO, JUBERE, JUSSI, JUSSUM. In the imperfect tenses of this verb, the U is, by exception, short.

UI, though generally treated as such in our Latin grammars, is certainly not a diphthong, the ear itself being judge. Pronounced with the stress of voice upon the first vowel, or equally distributed between the two, it is manifestly a dissyllable = *oo-ee;* or, if the stress be thrown upon the second (which is never the case with a proper diphthong) it becomes a monosyllable = *we;* the U, in this case, being necessarily regarded as a semi-consonant.

We give, then, the following scheme of the diphthongs in *common* use. Their pronunciation is determined at once and infallibly, by the well established sounds of the component elements.

AE (=AI)	sounds like	*ay*	the	Eng.	adv. of affirmation.
AU	"	"	*ow* in	"	*now.*
OE (=OI)	"	"	*oi* "	"	*Stoic*, or,
			oe "	"	*co-equal*, if pro-

nounced rapidly, the former as a monosyllable, and the latter as a dissyllable. It is nearly, but not quite equivalent to *oi* in the English *coil.*

This view of the Roman vowel and diphthongal systems will be found to throw much light upon many points of the language; *e. g.*, upon the question of the quantity of vowels in compounds and derivatives, and upon the entire subject of the composition and derivation of words. From the universal principle and practice of giving, in the sound of each diphthong, the two elementary sounds composing it, we can readily see how a diphthong, in a simple or primitive word, will often pass, in the compound or derivative, into the long sound of one of the two component elements, or into a long vowel closely related to one of the two sounds. Thus AE (= AI) passes into Ā or Ī, as, *e. g.*, AULĂĔBUS or AULĂĬBUS becomes AULĀBUS or AULĪBUS; from AD and QVAERO we have ACQVĪRO; from OB and CAEDO, OCCĪDO, etc. So also OI and OE are changed into Ō or Ī, and often into U, in consequence of the close approximation of the sounds O and U. Hence, from CON and EO, IRE, we have COÏTUS, then CO͡ITUS, then (without change of sound) COETUS, *a coming together*, *a meeting*, *an assembly*. Hence, we find in the early language LOEBER, and LOEBERTAS for LĪBER and LĪBERTAS, and at once see the reason of the long I. Comp. Ϝοῖκος, Ϝοῖνος, and VĪCUS, VĪNUM; so also we find anciently MOERUS, PLOIRUME, OINIVERSEI, OINOS, COMOINIS, COIRO, ARE, etc., for MŪRUS, PLŪRIME, ŪNĪVERSĪ, ŪNUS, COMMŪNIS, CŪRO, ARE, etc. Hence from PROVIDENS we have first (the V dropping out, as often when standing between two vowels), PROIDENS, then PRŪDENS; from JOVISGLANS, first JOVIGLANS, then JOIGLANS, then JŪGLANS; from CON and VINCTUS, COVINCTUS, COINCTUS, CŪNCTUS, "*all together;*" from MOVITO, ARE, freq. from MOVEO, ERE, we have MOITO, then MŪTO, ARE, *to move frequently, to change;* from NOVIPER, NŪPER; so from POENUS arose PŪNICUS, for which we find anciently both POENICUS and POINICUS. Comp. POENA (ποινή) and PŪNIO; MOENIA and MŪNIO, IRE; so also AU often passes into Ū, or its cognate Ō. Hence, CAUSA, INCŪSO; FRAUDO, DEFRŪDO; CLAUDO, RECLŪDO, etc.; so from SUB and FAUCES, *the throat,* SUFFŌCO, *to stop up the throat, to suffocate;* so PLŌSTRUM and LŌTUS, together with PLAUSTRUM and LAUTUS, CŌDEX, and CAUDEX, etc., etc. See Appendix, notes C and D.

To the student accustomed only to the English sounds of the vowels, and in the habit of giving to the broad, open sounds of AE and OE the slender sound of the Roman I, and to the AU the simple sound of *a* in *fall*, these changes seem unnatural and almost unaccountable. He can not see how AE and OE, having that slender sound, should pass, the one into Ā, and the other into Ō or Ū, or why AU should go into Ō or Ū. But he who is familiar with the true sounds of the Roman vowels and diphthongs will understand these changes the moment they strike his ear.

Again, the whole subject of quantity becomes, on this system, as simple as that one and one make two. The merest child can understand it. The distinction between long and short syllables is not nominal but real—not capricious and arbitrary but stable and rational. And a child who has been made familiar with the simple Roman system of vowel and diphthongal sounds will comprehend this distinction as readily as he will the difference between two and one. Indeed, precisely that is the distinction and the whole of it. It is well known that the Romans anciently expressed the long vowel sounds by the use of two vowel characters, and Quintilian informs us that this custom continued until after the time of Accius. On this system, then, we may dispense with the tedious, often conflicting and ever perplexing chapters on quantity with their interminable rules and exceptions, all made necessary, as we shall more fully show hereafter, by the attempt to reconcile things which are in themselves irreconcilable, viz., English vowel and diphthongal sounds and Latin quantities. Only let the pupil be taught from the first to give the proper sounds of the vowels and diphthongs, in *measure* as well as in *tone* (and they can be given in proper measure only with the Roman tone) and he will no more mistake the true quantity or accent of a word than the Romans themselves did. Let him only be taught to pronounce the language correctly, and he will intuitively deduce from the language itself its general rules of quantity. He will have that fine sense of quantity which will enable him to catch the rhythm of Latin poetry at once, and, as Horace says, to "mark the legitimate sounds with his *fingers* and *ear*." Mr. Walker gravely talks about "diphthongs to the *eye*," and the English system, as will be fully shown hereafter, actually converts all the common Roman diphthongs into these "ocular diphthongs," which are really no diphthongs at all; that is, they are not *two different vowel sounds in one syllable*, but simply *two vowel characters with one vowel sound.* But Horace knows of no such diphthongs; and Cicero says, "OMNIUM LONGITUDINUM ET BREVITATUM IN SONIS SICUT ACUTARUM GRAVIUMQVE VOCUM JUDICIUM, NATURA IN AURIBUS NOSTRIS COLLOCAVIT."

On the other hand, to teach the student, from his first entrance upon the study of Latin, the English system of pronunciation; to get him thoroughly habituated to this false method, and then to attempt, by lodging in his brain some verbal rules of quantity and prosody at war often with each other and commonly with his pronunciation, to make him appreciate and observe the rhythm of Latin poetry, is like keeping a child in a rude society, where all the laws of a pure and finished language are habitually violated, until his habits of thought and speech are completely formed and confirmed, and then expecting him, by virtue of his committing to memory the common rules of grammar and rhetoric, to talk at once with grammatical and rhetorical correctness and elegance.

Again, this view of the vowels and diphthongs will also explain how the four vowel declensions, commonly called the first, second, fourth and fifth declensions, sprang from the one original declension which has been retained most fully in what is now commonly called the *third*, but which should be called the *consonant declension* in distinction from the other four. The case endings of this original declension are as follows, viz.:

	SINGULAR.	PLURAL.
Nom.	S, or M,*	ĔS.
Gen.	IS,	ĔRUM.
Dat.	I,	ĔBUS or ĬBUS.
Acc.	M,	ĔS.
Voc.	like nom.	ĔS.
Abl.	E,	ĔBUS or ĬBUS.

When these endings, all of them, except the nominative, accusative, and vocative singular, commencing with or consisting of a vowel, were attached to roots ending in a vowel, there arose by syncopation, contraction and elision, various changes which produced the four varieties of declension properly termed the A, E, O and U declensions, according as the roots end in those vowels respectively. Hence, *e. g.*, FAMILIA, FAMILIA-IS, FAMILIA-I, FAMILIA-M, FAMILIA; FAMILIA-E. In the genitive we have sometimes a contraction of the AI into Ā, giving us FAMILIĀS, as in PATERFAMILIĀS; generally the S is dropped, leaving AÏ, as in the trissyllables still

* S generally for *personal*, and M for *impersonal* nouns.

found in the poets, AULAÏ, AQVAÏ, etc.; at other times, the AI are united, giving us AULÂI, a dissyllable; and finally the I is supplanted by E without change of sound. Thus we get the first or A declension as follows, viz.:

SINGULAR.

Originally.	*Finally.*
AULĂ,	AULĂ.
AULĂ-IS, AULĀS, AULAÏ, AULÂI, or	AULAE.
AULĂ-I,	AULAE.
AULĂ-M,	AULĂM.
AULĂ,	AULĂ.
AULĂ-E,	AULĀ.

PLURAL.

AULĂ-ĔS,	(*s*, dropped)	AULAE.
AULĂ-ĔRUM,	(contracted)	AULĀRUM.
AULĂ-ĔBUS or ĬBUS,	(con. and sync.)	AULĪS.
AULĂ-ĔS,	(contracted)	AULĂS.
AULĂ-ĔS,	(*s*, dropped)	AULAE.
AULĂ-ĔBUS or ĬBUS,	(con. and sync.)	AULĪS.

The dative and ablative plural are first contracted into AULĀBUS or AULĪBUS (both which forms are still occasionally retained,) and the latter is then syncopated and still further contracted into AULĪS, just as

QVIBUS goes occasionally into QVIS, and as HIBUS, the old dative and ablative plural of HIC, has passed into HIS.

We see at once, from the above, why the ultimate of the ablative singular is *long*, though final A in words declined is elsewhere *short*—why the accusative plural AS is *long*, while the accusative singular AM is *short*—why the penult of the genitive plural is *long*, and why the ultimate of the dative and ablative plural is *long*, though final IS, is generally *short*, etc. In the same way, we might explain, with equally satisfactory results, the development both of the other vowel declensions from the original declension, and also of the three vowel conjugations (with roots ending respecively in A, E, and I,) as distinguished from the third or consonant conjugation; but it is unnecessary here to go through with the details.

Now to the Roman-Latinist all these changes are simple and natural, while the English-Latinist *without going out of his system*, could never even discover them.

C.

SOUNDS OF THE CONSONANTS.

The main differences between the Roman and English systems in sounding the consonants are limited to the letters C, G, QV, J, S, and T. I need not, therefore, speak particularly of the other consonants.

The original Roman alphabet of sixteen letters, as borrowed from the Greeks, did not contain the letter G; but the C occupied the place of the Greek Γ, and corresponded to it nearly in form and precisely in sound, as the K did to the Greek *kappa*. Hence, in the earlier times, we find uniformly LECIONES, MACISTRATOS, PUCNANDO, etc., instead of LEGIONES, MAGISTRATUS, PUGNANDO, etc. See Aristarchus, De Arte Gram., i., 18, SUB FIN.

The C, however, was early hardened into the sound of K, and, by degrees, actually supplanted the K in all the words of the language except KALENDAE and the proper names KAESO and KARTHAGO. It became necessary therefore to employ a new character to represent the sound of γ; and for this purpose the G was formed by appending the mark (ι) to the C. Thenceforth, so long as the Latin remained a living tongue, the simple C was the sign of the hard

K-sound (= Greek κ), and the modified C or G was the sign of the soft K-sound (= Greek γ). Nor is there the least evidence that they were ever employed for any other purpose.

In the golden age of the Latin, the Greeks and Romans, who were perfectly familiar with each other's language, regarded the C and the Greek κ, the G and the Greek γ as entirely equivalent. When the Romans wrote Greek words in Latin characters, they used C to represent κ before the vowels E and I, as well as before the other vowels and the liquids; as CECROPS, Κέκροψ; CILICIA, Κιλικία. The Greeks, on the other hand, used their κ for the Roman C in all cases; since in writing Latin names they write the syllables, CE, CI, with κ and not with ς; as, Κικέρων, CICERO; Σκιπίων, SCIPIO. Suidas, speaking of the C worn on the shoes of Roman Senators, calls it τὸ Ρωμαϊκὸν κάππα. See Aristarchus, DE ARTE GRAM., LIB. i., c. xvii. The Romans wrote Γερύων, GERYON; γίγας, GIGAS. The Greeks wrote VIRGILIUS, Οὐιργίλιος. A passage in St. Augustine furnishes positive evidence that the Greek γ, and the Roman G, were pronounced alike even before the vowel E. He says, "CUM DICO LEGE, IN HIS DUABUS SYLLABIS, ALIUD GRAECUS, ALIUD LATINUS

INTELLIGIT," thus clearly showing that the Latin LEGE and the Greek λέγε had the same sound.

The fact, too, that the union of either C or G with S always produces X, shows that both are gutturals, as, *e. g.*, PAX from root PAC, and nominative ending S; REX from REG and S. See App., Note. I.

Again, we have in syncopated words proof that C and G invariably retained their guttural sound; as in the supines of DOCERE and FACERE. If the C had the sound of S, the supines would have been pronounced DOSĒTUM, FASĬTUM and the syncopated forms would naturally have been DOSTUM, FASTUM, not DOCTUM, FACTUM. If the G of LEGI had the sound of the English J, the supine LEGITUM must have been pronounced LEJITUM, and the syncopated form could not have been LECTUM.

Again, we have TRICESIMUS and TRIGESIMUS from TRIGINTA; QVADRINGENTI for QVADRINCENTI; DECIMUS and DECUMUS from DECEM. Now unless the C and G were invariably gutturals before E and I as well as before the other vowels, such orthographical changes could not have taken place. We must suppose that the C in DECIMUS, DECUMUS and DECEM had one uniform sound corresponding to that of the K in *δέκα*.

On this point, also, the testimony of the Latin

grammarians is full and conclusive. In the discussion of the question whether the K was to be numbered among the letters of the Roman alphabet the Latin writers make the most explicit declarations of the perfect identity of the C and K in regard to the sound they represented. Quintilian, on the ground of this identity, condemns the use of K in writing Latin words.

"NAM K QVIDEM IN NULLIS VERBIS UTENDUM PUTO . . (HOC EO NON OMISI QVOD QVIDAM EAM, QVOTIES A SEQVATUR, NECESSARIAM CREDUNT;) CUM SIT C LITERA, QVAE AD OMNES VOCALES VIM SUAM PERFERAT." LIB. i., vii. 10.

Priscian agrees with Quintilian in regarding the K as superfluous.

"K ENIM ET Q QVAMVIS FIGURA ET NOMINE VIDEANTUR ALIQVAM HABERE DIFFERENTIAM, CUM C TAMEN EANDEM TAM IN SONO VOCUM QVAM IN METRO, CONTINENT POTESTATEM. ET K QVIDEM PENITUS SUPERVACUA EST; NULLA ENIM RATIO VIDETUR, CUR, A SEQUENTE, K SCRIBI DEBEAT." LIB. i., c. iv.

And again:

"QVAMVIS IN VARIA FIGURA ET VARIO NOMINE SINT K ET Q ET C TAMEN, QVIA UNAM VIM HABENT TAM IN METRO QVAM IN SONO, PRO UNA LITERA ACCIPI DEBENT." LIB. i., c. iv.

"K SUPERVACUA EST, UT SUPRA DIXIMUS; QVAE QVAMVIS SCRIBATUR, NULLAM ALIAM VIM HABET QVAM C." LIB. i., c. viii. See further, Appendix, notes E and F.

We may be sure then that the Roman C and G corresponded precisely and uniformly with the Greek κ and γ.

Q appears only before V, and QV only before a Latin vowel. In the classical period of the language, QV as a compound character, represents invariably a simple consonant sound; never creates position; is often interchanged with C; and had, according to the statements of the Latin grammarians, precisely the same sound with the C and K. In addition to the authorities already quoted, see Aristarchus, DE ARTE GRAM., LIB. i., CAP. xviii., who states explicitly that the C, K and Q have the same sound, and that the V after Q is silent. Cicero makes a pun, in which COQVE, the voc. of COQVUS, *a cook*, and the adverb QVOQVE, *also*, must have been assumed to be sounded alike. QVOTIDIE and COTIDIE, QVUM and CUM, COQVI and COCI, COLLIQVIAS and COLLICIAS were different modes of spelling the same words, both in common use at the same period of time, and must therefore have been pronounced alike. The Romans also frequently wrote

SEQVUTUS and SECUTUS, LOQVUTUS and LOCUTUS; from QVATIO we have CONCUTIO, where V represents the A and C the QV of the simple verb; and from RELINQVO we have RELI(N)CTUS, RELICTUS; again the QV, like any other guttural, combined with S forms X, *e. g.*, COQV|O, COQV|ERE, COX|I, COC|TUM; again, all adjectives whose roots end in a vowel are compared by the use of MAGIS and MAXIME, but those whose roots end in QV are not so compared, *e. g.*, IDONE|US, MAGIS IDONE|US, MAXIME IDONE|US, but ANTIQV|US, ANTIQV|IOR, ANTIQV|ISSIMUS. Hence in the triliteral word QVA, QVE, QVI, QVO, QVU, the QV has always the simple sounds of C or K. In the genitive and dative singular of QVIS or QVI, viz., CUJUS or CUIUS and CUI, the U represents not the U of the nominative, but the O which is found in the old orthography QVOIUS and QVOI, and the C represents the QV of the nominative. The substitution of C for QV in this word took place in Quintilian's time. He tells us that, in his youth, the dative was still written QVOI. The genitive therefore is to be pronounced *kōō-yŏŏs*, and the dative either as a dissyllable *kŏŏ-ĕe*, or more commonly as a monosyllable in which the U passes over into a consonant sound resembling our W, *kwee*. But the nominative is *kee*. The English system, with characteristic perversity, reverses this rule and mispronounces both the QV of the nominative and CU of the dative, to say nothing of its false sound of the vowel. Upon such general grounds, we might be sure of the Roman pronunciation of the genitive and dative of this pronoun; and I was in the habit myself of pronouncing the nominative *kee* and the dative *kwee* for many years before I noticed an incidental remark of Priscian, which shows very clearly how the Romans pronounced them. After stating that C, K and Q were identical in sound, and that K was therefore superfluous, he adds that the Q as well as the K would be superfluous, but that it seems to distinguish words in which the V was silent—as in QVI—from those in which it was pronounced, as in CUI. L. i., c. iv. That the real difference between the pronunciation of QVI and CUI was anciently observed in England, is proved by the directions given by Beda in his treatise on orthography. "Q LITERA TUNC RECTE PONITUR CUM ILLI STATIM U LITERA ET ALIA QVAELIBET PLURESVE VOCALES CONIUNCTAE FUERINT ITA UT UNA SYLLABA FIAT; CAETERA PER C SCRIBUNTUR. QVI SYLLABA PER QVI SCRIBITUR; SI DIVIDITUR, PER CUI SCRIBENDA EST." So HUIC the dative of HIC, is either *hŏŏ-ĕĕc* or *hwēēc*. LO-QVOR, SE-QVOR are dissyllables, but they were sometimes written LO-CŬ-

OR, SÉ-CŬ-OR, when they were trissyllables, from which we have LO-CŬ-Ĭ-TUS, SE-CŬ-Ĭ-TUS, and contracted LO-CŪ-TUS, SE-CŪ-TUS. There is not the slightest doubt, then, that in the classical times, QV represents the simple guttural or K-sound.* See Appendix, note G.

* In regard to the characters C, K, QV, it is natural to inquire, first, Why did the Romans, the notation of whose language is in general so simple and regular, employ these three characters to represent one and the same sound (= Greek κ)? and second, How are we to account for the fact that the V after Q is invariably silent and without significance in the classical period of the language?

The first question admits of a ready answer. In the Latin, as in other ancient languages, *e. g.*, the Hebrew and the Greek, several of the letters appear to have had a syllabic power. One character, was used to denote the syllable KA, another KO, and so on. These two characters were called in Hebrew *kaph* and *koph*, and in Greek, *kappa* and *koppa*, the names of these letters thus indicating their syllabic nature and use. After they lost this syllabic power, they were still employed as signs of the same initial consonant sounds, but were restricted, for a time, each to a connection with the vowel of the syllable it originally represented. The Greek kappa, *e. g.*, after it ceased to be syllabic in power, was nevertheless used, for a time, only before the vowel *a*, and *koppa* only before the *o*-sound; but eventually, one of them becoming thus superfluous, the *koppa* disappeared from the alphabet, and the *kappa* was employed before all vowels. So in Latin, K originally denoted the syllable KA, and, after it ceased to be syllabic, was never used before any vowel but A; so Q was used only before V, and C before E, I and O. The name of the K, viz., KA (*a* as in father), and of the Q, viz., QV, (= *koo*) clearly indicates the nature and use of each. And our names of these and other letters are relics of this same usage, only we have corrupted the vowel sound. We call *k*, *ka* (*a* as

I, when used as a consonant, or J as it has commonly been written within the last two centuries, had the sound of our Y, as it has in German. This was the natural result of the hardening of the

in made,) and not *ke* which would better accord with *be, ce, de,* etc., the names of *b, c, d,* etc., and we call *q, ku,* only changing the vowel sound from *oo* to *u* as in *tube.* The Anglo-Saxons, undoubtedly, pronounced the *ka* and *ku* as the Romans did, and the Germans do, = *kah* and *koo.*

Now just as in Greek the *koppa* became superfluous, and disappeared from the alphabet, so in Latin, after C became established as a hard K-sound, the K became superfluous and virtually disappeared. KAPUT, KALUMNIA, etc., became CAPUT, CALUMNIA, etc. The K was retained only in the three words already mentioned, and in certain abbreviations. One mode of abbreviation common among the Romans, furnishes an illustration of the original custom of giving to the letters a syllabic power. This consisted in denoting a syllable by a single consonant whenever the vowel of this syllable was identical with that by which the consonant was pronounced in the alphabet. Thus B stood for the syllable BE; BNE stood for BENE; so D for DE; and DCIMUS for DECIMUS; so Q for QV, and QID, QAE, for QVID, QVAE; so C stood for the syllable CE; but as the vowel A was contained in the name of K, this letter was used to denote the syllable CA; thus CRA would be read CERA; but KRA, CARA. See Appendix, note H. There remain, then, in ordinary use in Latin, only C and Q or QV, as the representatives of the hard K-sound.

How then, the second question is, did this V become invariably silent and without significance? This usage arose, I think, from the singular fact that the QV, unlike either the CE, CI, CO, or KA, were employed only before a vowel. The V after Q must originally have been sounded; as a vowel = *oo,* and as a consonant = *w.* QVAM, *e. g.,* must originally have been pronounced as a dissyllable *koo-am,* and as a monosyllable, which it ordinarily was, *kwam.* But when the QV stood before another vowel sound I before another vowel. IAM may be either a dissyllable or a monosyllable, according as the I is used as a vowel or a consonant. It is, therefore, either EE-AM, or, when the two syllables

V, the two short vowels would naturally unite to form a long one. Just as AMAABAM, though so written till near the time of Cicero, was nevertheless a trissyllable, pronounced AMABAM, so QVVM, which might be a dissyllable, *koo-oom*, would ordinarily be a monosyllable, and pronounced *koom* rather than *kwoom*. Now, if the Romans could have reduced the written characters QVVM to QVM, as they did AMAARE to AMARE, DOCEERE to DOCERE, etc., they would unquestionably have done it, and then, when the letters had lost their syllabic power, and C had become established as a hard K-sound, the C would, in all probability, have entirely supplanted the Q and the Q *alone*, as it did the K, while the single V following it, would have retained its sound and significance as a vowel, and the syllables of the words in which the C thus took the place of Q would have been unchanged. But as they could write only QVVM (and not QVM) and this was ordinarily pronounced *koom*, the attempt to reduce the word to the written *form* of a monosyllable would naturally result in the substitution of C for QV, *i. e.*, CVM, for QVVM. Thus the C would be *apparently* identical with QV. Then again, as the O and U-sounds were closely allied, and the two characters frequently interchanged, as SERVOS and SERVUS, QVOR and QVUR (subsequently, CUR) the QVO, also, would naturally be sounded as a monosyllable, KO, not KWO, and we should have QVOTIDIE and COTIDIE, two common contemporaneous orthographies with one pronunciation. Now just in proportion as these orthographic variations, these interchanges of C and QV became more numerous and frequent, the original power of the QV would be gradually modified in the popular conception and pronunciation until it became, in the classical times, actually equivalent to the simple C before all vowels; so that QVA, QVE, QVI, would be pronounced like KA, KE, KI, as well as QVO and QVU like KO and KU.

are run into one by a rapid pronunciation, becomes inevitably YAM, and the compound ETIAM is sometimes a trissyllable, ET-EE-AM, but generally a dissyllable, ET-YAM. So PARIES is either PĂ-RĬ-ĔS (pronounced, PĂ-REE-ĂCE) or PAR-YES (pronounced PÁR-YĂCE); PARIETE is either PA-RÍ-E-TE or PÁR-YĔ-TE; POMPEIUS is either POM-PÉ-I-US or POM-PÉ-YUS, etc.

S is always a sharp sibilant like the Greek Σ, and is sounded as in the English *sin*. The Latin MŪSĂ then corresponds in sound precisely with the Greek *μοῦσα*. The Romans, by the way, uniformly represent the Greek *ου* by their V, and the Greeks the Latin V by their *ου*. CATŬLUS, in which, as Klotz states, the penult vowel was so short as scarcely to be heard, was translated thus into Greek, Κάτλους.

T always preserves its pure sound, RATIO=RĂ-TEE-O; ARTIUM = ĂR-TEE-OOM; JUSTITIA = YOOS-TEE-TEE-Ă; etc., etc.

F and H, I may remark in passing, were originally mere marks of aspiration, the former for the *spiritus lenis* (the Æolic digamma F) the latter for the *spiritus asper*. The form of the latter resulted from the union of the two Grecian breathing marks ꟻ and ⅃. They were afterwards treated as letters, and together with G introduced between E and I. The originally soft F was, however, hardened, and passed over almost into the sound of the Greek Φ. Hence FABIUS = Φάβιος, φυγή = FUGA; while the breathing previously indicated by F was subsequently expressed by V when used as a consonant. The H besides its use in the beginning of aspirated syllables, and between two vowels in the middle of a word (*e. g.*, VEHEMENS), was employed also after the consonants C, P, T, R, to aspirate them. This usage appears originally in Grecian words where CH, PH, TH, RH, answer to the Greek χ, φ, θ, ῥ.

With these remarks on the consonants whose Roman pronunciation differed from the English, we may proceed to the

DIVISION OF THE CONSONANTS.

They are divided first into *simple* and *double* consonants.

The *simple* consonants are distinguished,

1.) According to the different organs which are particularly active in their formation; as

Throat-letters, *gutturals;* G, C (QV,) CH, R, H

Tongue-letters, *linguals;* D, T, TH, L, N, J, S.

Lip-letters, *labials;* B, P, PH, F, M, V.

2.) According to the nature of the action of the

organs in their formation, or according to *certain degrees of articulation*, as

a.) *Mutes*, *i. e.*, such as are formed by the strongest effort of the vocal organs, or, are *most perfectly articulated.* These are either,

Soft (*mediae*), G, D, B,
Hard (*tenues*); C (QV), T, P;
Rough (*aspiratae*); CH, TH, PH, F.

b.) *Semi-vowels*, *i. e.*, consonants which, in respect to the action of the vocal organs, approach *most nearly to the vowels.* These again are subdivided into

α.) *Liquids*; *i. e.*, those which readily flow or unite with the mutes; L, M, N, R.

β.) *Spirants*, those which are formed by the breath or voice *most slightly interrupted*; H, J, S, V.

{ By the breath, H, S.
{ " " voice, J, V.

In accordance with these distinctions we give the following tabular view of the simple consonants, exhibiting the two grounds of classification. The mutes belonging to the three organs, *the throat*, *the tongue* and *the lips* are called respectively the K-, T-, and P-sounds.

LETTERS OF THE SAME ORGAN.

LETTERS OF LIKE ARTICULATION.

	Gutturals.	Linguals.	Labials.
1. Mutes.	(K-Sound.)	(T-Sound.)	(P-Sound.)
A) soft	G	D	B
B) hard	C (QV)	T	P
C) rough	CH	TH	PH, F
2. Liquids.	R	L, N	M
3. Spirants.	H	J, S	V

The hard and soft mutes are sometimes properly distinguished as *surds* and *sonants*, the term *surd* being applied to those letters whose articulation is preceded by an entire interruption of the voice; and the term *sonant* to those which are accompanied by an audible murmuring of the voice. Thus C, T, P, are surds; G, D, B, sonants.

The *double* consonants are,

X from CS, GS, QVS, rarely HS;

Z from DS or SD.

The former is the only genuine Latin double consonant. The latter belongs properly to no Latin word, but is found only in Greek words and in some proper nouns borrowed from foreign languages, *e. g.*, ZONA, ZAMA.

The aspirates CH, TH, PH are originally foreign to the language. They appear, therefore, chiefly in words borrowed from the Greek, although even many of these were deprived of the aspiration. Only in a few common nouns, as PULCHER, SEPULCHRUM, the CH is used instead of C. It occurs also in a few proper nouns, as GRACCHUS. TH occurs also in some proper nouns, as CETHEGUS, SPINTHER, OTHO, CARTHAGO. Elsewhere it was not used in native words. F was frequently written instead of PH, even in nouns derived from the Greek. PHASELUS, PHALERAE, DELPHINUS were frequently written FASELUS, FALERAE, DELFINUS, etc. Instead of TRIUMPHUS (*θριάμβος*) the original orthography was TRIUMPUS.

The aspirated R (RH) is retained in words from the Greek in which ῥ stood at the beginning of a word or after another ῥ, and hence we have RHYTHMUS, RHETOR, PARRHASIUS. Also several words of barbarian origin were written with RH, as RHENUS, RHODANUS, RHEDA.

F, in the best times, corresponded more or less closely to the Greek *θ*, as is evident from Quintilian 12, 10, 29. It is strictly therefore the only aspirated mute among the sounds of the Latin language.

Such, in its admirable simplicity, symmetry and completeness, was the system according to which the Romans themselves pronounced their noble language: a system ascertained and established not only by its interior harmony with all the parts of its structure, and all the facts of its historical development, but also, in every important particular, by the testimony of its own grammarians, and the concurrent opinions of the best Latin scholars of modern times. With this system before us, we are prepared to justify the twofold charge which we have brought against the present English method of Latin pronunciation: (1.) that it thoroughly perverts and vitiates its elementary sounds, thereby destroying its euphony and greatly obscuring the facts and principles of its derivation and composition; and (2.) that it absolutely compels the violation of its quantities, and renders impossible a right reading of its verse.

And first, how utterly at variance the English method is with that above detailed must be obvious at a glance to every observer. It gives to every vowel, and also to many of the consonants, sounds which are radically different, not only from those of the Romans, but also from each other; and to every diphthong, a sound not merely different from that of the Romans, but entirely incompatible with the fundamental principle of the Roman diphthongal system. A character which, in one position, represents the short sound of one vowel, in another position, may represent the long sound of another vowel. Thus in SĂGĂ, *a mantle*, the first A is pronounced as E long, the second as A short; in DĔCĔM, the first E is pronounced as I long, the second as E short; in CĪCĬ, the long and short vowels are both made long with the sound of the diphthong AI; but in the adjective CĪCĬNUS, the first I, which is still long, is made short with the entirely different sound of I in *pin;* in NŌVI, the long O has its proper sound, but in its derivative, NŌBILIS, the long O is made short, with a different sound wholly unknown to the Latin language; in FŬO, FŬI, the Ŭ is made long; in FŪR, the Ū is made short, and the sound radically changed.

Again, this system gives to simple vowels the sound of diphthongs, and to diphthongs that of simple vowels and even of *short* vowels, though a diphthong is always long and always admitted to be so by the English-Latinist himself. The I of DICO is pronounced AI, the AE of CAEDO, I; in the compound PRAECĪDO the diphthong and the simple vowel I are made to change places; the diphthong in CAESAR has the sound of I long; in CAESARIS, that of E short. Not one of the Latin diphthongs is, on the English system, pronounced as a diphthong, except EI (which occurs in only three or four words) and *that* is *mis*-pronounced. AE and OE have the simple vowel sound of the English *e*, either long or short, as in *mete* or *met;* AU, that of the simple *a* in *fall;* EU that of *u* in *tube.* So much for the perversion of the pure sounds of the Latin vowels and diphthongs. Not one of them has escaped the contaminating touch of the English system.

But the system does, perhaps, even greater violence to some of the consonant sounds. C, always with the Romans, a hard guttural mute, which is one of the most important consonants in a language, often becomes a mere lingual spirant, either hard or soft, *i. e.*, it becomes either the hard or soft sibilant, S or Z. G, always a soft guttural, is changed into a lingual or dento-lingual, representing one of the most unpleasant sounds in our language, and one which is wholly foreign to the Latin, that of J, or DG. So, again, the J consonant (English *y*) is made to represent the same harsh sound. In JUNG|O, JUNG|ERE, JUNX|I, JUNC|TUM, pronounced *Latine*, there is not a disagreeable sound, and each letter represents here, as elsewhere, but one sound; but it is impossible to imagine a more unpleasant combination of sounds than is heard when those words are pronounced *Anglice*. So again, the sound required to be given to SI and TI when followed by a vowel, as in RATIO, OFFENSIO, pronounced RASHEO, OFFENSHEO, is wholly alien from the Latin, and offensive to every refined ear. In view of these corruptions of Latin vowels, diphthongs and consonants, it must be admitted, I think, by every candid mind, that the English mode of Latin pronunciation has forced into that language a vast number of harsh and discordant sounds which greatly mar its really beautiful and euphonious character.

Nor does this system do violence merely to the euphony of the language. The changes which we make in the sounds of the consonants, especially of the gutturals and of J, introduce a great number of irregularities and anomalies of pronunciation, which, besides being wholly foreign to the language, obscure the relation of derivatives to each other and to their primitive; of compound to simple terms; of different cases of the same noun, or tenses of the same verb to each other and to their common root. These changes are sometimes so wanton and absurd that nothing but the force of habit, established from our infancy in the use of our vernacular tongue, could reconcile us to them. For instance, in verbs which are reduplicated in the perfect, we form the reduplication by using a consonant sound totally different from that of the initial letter of the verb-root, and also change the sound of that letter itself. From CĂ-NO, instead of CÉ-CĬ-NI (KÉ-KĬ-NI) we have SÉS-I-NI; from CĂ-DO, instead of CÉ-CĬ-DI (KÉ-KĬ-DI) we have SES-I-DI; from CAE-DO, instead of CE-CĪ-DI (KE-KĪ-DI) we have SES-Ī-DI. But perhaps the absurdity of such changes is nowhere more apparent than in many compound verbs where the final consonant of the preposition is assimilated to the initial of the verb, as in ACCĬPIO, OCCĬDO and OCCĪDO. How beautifully and clearly does the pronunciation, AKKĬPIO, ÓKKĬDO and OKKĪDO point out the elements AD and CĂPIO, OB and CĂDO, and OB and CAĒDO! But, on the English system, after we have changed the sound of the verb's initial from a guttural to the sharp sibilant s, we do not allow the preposition, either to recover its original final letter, or, by way of assimilation, to assume a sibilant. We say neither AD-SIPIO, nor AS-SIPIO, but AK-SIPIO; neither OB-SIDO, nor OS-SIDO, but OK-SIDO, etc.

3*

Again, by this practice of capriciously changing the sounds of the consonants according to the vowel following them, a slight inflectional or other variation in the spelling of a word, the elision or transposition of a single letter are enough to make an entirely new word of it. The cases of AMICUS pronounced *Anglice*, without stopping here to notice the radical changes of vowel sounds, are as follows:

AMIKUS,	AMISI,
AMISI,	AMIKORUM,
AMIKO,	AMISIS,
AMIKUM,	AMIKOS,
AMISE,	AMISI,
AMIKO.	AMISIS.

What a regular and beautiful variety! Nor have we variety merely, but confusion. How is it possible, for example, to distinguish the genitive singular, and nominative and vocative plural, from the perfect of the verb AMITTO? Who, again, would ever imagine that FAC and DIC had come, by elision, from FASE and DISE? or NEC from NEKWE? Who would suppose CERTUS, and CRETUS, as we pronounce them, to be different forms of the same participle? For it must be borne in mind that such elisions and metatheses are part of the history of the living language, occurring not in the use of the learned or on the written page, but in the *mouth* of the people. Such illustrations of the confusion created by these capricious and radical changes of consonant sounds might be multiplied AD LIBITUM. But those already furnished are sufficient for our present purpose.

Again, this corruption of Latin pronunciation has erected a high wall of partition between the Latin and its kindred languages—a wall which very few Latin students, accustomed only to the English method, have ever attempted, and fewer still have been able, to scale—a wall which entirely shuts out from the view of the exclusive English pronouncer a large majority of the ethnical affinities of the Latin language. What mere English Latinist would be likely to discover the relation, *e. g.*, between ACOETIS (pronounced *a-sée-tis*) and the Greek ἄκοιτις? between CERCŪRUS (*sur-cū-rus*) and κέρκουρος? between CĪCĬ (*sai-sai*) and κίκι? between CĬCĬNUS (*sis-i-nus*) and κίκινος? between COENA (*see-na*) and κοῖνος? between CELLA (*sella*) and the German KELLER? between CISTA (*sista*) and KISTE? between CICER (*sai-ser*) and KICHER? between CINC-TUM (*sink-tum*) and the English *kink*? between TUM-ULUS and *tomb*? etc., etc.

The Greek, which is so closely allied to the Latin, but which has suffered far less than the Latin from these corruptions, becomes to our English-Latinist a very strange language, rather than a sister of the same family. He has learned, *e. g.*, to pronounce the Latin OCEĂNUS, *o-shée-a-nu* or still more erroneously, *o-shee-á-nus;* he meets the Greek word ὠκεᾰνὸς and thinks it quite an alien, but the Roman Latinist finds the two words pronounced precisely alike, (except a slight difference between the o and ʊ,) and perceives at once their identity; the English Latinist is staggered at the difference between CILICIA (*Sai-lish-y-a*) and KILIKÍA, but the Roman Latinist sees no difference at all. Just so in hundreds of other instances which might be named. But this point will be more fully illustrated in another place.

Having thus substantiated, as I think, the statement that the English system of Latin pronunciation thoroughly perverts the pure sounds of the language, and having shown some of the pernicious effects of that perversion in introducing harshness, irregularity and confusion, into a language which, in itself, is eminently euphonious, symmetrical and philosophical, I proceed to the remaining charge, viz., that this system not merely tolerates, but enjoins the violation of the true quantities of the language, and, consequently, of the just measure of Latin verse. We concede to the English system that it makes this stern demand of the sacrifice of Latin quantity "not willingly, but of necessity." Such is its *nature*, it can not do otherwise. It possesses an inherent and ineradicable incompatibility with the proper Latin quantities, and with the whole theory of Roman verse. It may be thought a bold and arrogant statement, and yet we will have both the courage and the frankness to make it, that no man can read, on the English method, any ten consecutive lines of Latin poetry of any considerable length, say dactylic hexameters, without violating Latin quantity at least as many as twenty-five or thirty times, and frequently twice or thrice thirty times. We sometimes meet with the striking inconsistency of an earnest stickler for the English method, who plumes himself upon his achievements and skill in this matter of Latin quantity, and manifests a self-righteous horror of what he calls "false quantity," but who nevertheless unconsciously makes one or more false quantities in nearly every Latin word he utters. The fault as well as the inconsistency belong not so much to the individual as to the system, a system which, at the same time, both forces its practitioner into error, and blinds him to its existence. To this point it becomes necessary for us to give special attention, in order to set forth in its true light the immeasurable superiority of the Roman over the English system of Latin pronunciation. By "false quantity" the pronouncer of Latin on the English system, or the English pronouncer, as I will briefly call him, means simply "false accentuation" of a word from non-observance of the quantity of its penultimate syllable. The quantity of the other syllables he is indifferent to, and, by the necessities of his system, is perpetually violating. Only place the *accent* on the right syllable of a word, and our adept English pronouncer will pronounce you "all right" in the matter of quantity, though you give, as on the English system you may, a false quantity to every syllable in it. Take, *e. g.*, the word FRIGIDIS. The penult being short, the accent is on the antepenult. But the ultimate and antepenultimate vowels are long; yet our English-Latinist doesn't say *frāi-jĕ-dāis* but *frĭj-e-dĭs*, making the first and last syllables short instead of long, and thus robbing the word of two fifths of its quantity; in FĀBŬLĪS, though he give the right accent, he makes the two long syllables short and the short one long.

This disregard of quantity, except so far as quantity determines the place of the accent, the English-Latinist constantly exhibits. The Latin Grammar of Andrews and Stoddard, which is, perhaps, most commonly used in this country, contains the following: "To pronounce Latin words correctly, it is necessary to ascertain the quantities of their last two syllables only; and the rules for the quantities of final syllables would be unnecessary, but for the occasional addition of enclitics. As these are generally monosyllables, and, for the purpose of accentuation, are considered as parts of the words to which they are annexed, they cause the final syllable of the original word to become the penult of the compound. It is necessary, therefore, to learn the quantities of those final syllables *only* which end in a *vowel*." This quotation gives us the pith of the whole doctrine of the English system on the subject of Latin quantity. The quantity of the penultimate syllable is ordinarily all we need to know in order "*to pronounce Latin words correctly*." Now the truth is, that to read Latin, and especially Latin poetry, correctly, we must give each syllable of each word its just measure of sound. Cicero informs us, that the Romans, even in their common discourse, were very careful to mark the quantity of every syllable. And think we that the *poet* was indifferent to the quantity of a single syllable introduced into his verse? Is it not the regulated succession of long and short syllables, and not, as in English, of accented and unaccented syllables, which constitutes the rhythm of Latin poetry? Cicero tells us, De Orat., L. iii., c. 48, that the Roman poet was so strictly controlled by the laws of measure that not a syllable in his verse might be, by the smallest breath even, longer or shorter than was proper. Even if the poet had been disposed to admit the slightest violation of the proper measure, the people, as Cicero states in the same book, c. 50, would not allow him to do it; he says that those who were entirely ignorant of the rules of versification had so nice and intuitive a sense of the true syllabic measures, that they would raise a clamor against the dramatic poet, if he made a single syllable either longer or shorter than was just. How then can *we* give the real rhythm of a Latin verse without observing the true quantity of each syllable of it? It is obviously impossible. We have, then, two impossible things. First, it is impossible for the English-Latinist not to violate

Latin quantity, perpetually; and second, it is impossible to preserve Latin rhythm without observing Latin quantity, uniformly.

Before proceeding further with this point, we would request the reader to bear in mind that, on the English system of Latin pronunciation, A long sounds like *a* in *made*, A short, like *a* in *mat*; E long, like *e* in *mete*, E short, like *e* in *met*; I long, like *i* in *pine*, I short, like *i* in *pin*; O long, like *o* in *note*, O short, like *o* in *not*; U long, like *u* in *tube*, U short, like *u* in *tub*. Now it will be found, upon examination, that it is only in words having the penult vowel long, and followed by a single consonant, that we are sure, on this system, of having the quantity of even one syllable correctly given; and that, in all other words, whether dissyllables with short penult, or polysyllables with accented antepenults, every syllable may have a false quantity. TŬ-BĪS, *e. g.*, the dative plural of TŬ-BĂ, is pronounced TŪ-BĬS; RĒ-GŬ-LĪS, dative of RĒ-GŬ-LĂ, is pronounced RĔG-Ū-LĬS. In words of two syllables, the English rule lengthens the penult vowel when followed by a single consonant, whatever be its real quantity; and in words of more than two syllables having the antepenult accented, it shortens the accented syllable, whatever its quantity, except

(1st) in the case of U, and (2d) in those words in which the vowel of the penult is followed by another vowel. In these, the rule lengthens the accented antepenult, whatever its quantity, unless the vowel of the accented syllable be I, which is invariably shortened, whatever its quantity. In an accented antepenultimate syllable, then, the I is always short, and the U always long, whatever be their real quantity. In accordance, then, with the above rules, PĂTER, MĔRUS, MĬSER, MŎLA, NŬRUS, become PĀTER, MĒRUS, MĪSER, MŌLA, NŪRUS: FĀBULOR, RĒGULA, DĪLIGO, NŌBILIS, become FĂBULOR, RĔGULA, DĬLIGO, NŎBILIS; but DŬBITO becomes DŪBITO: MĂNEO, SĔDEO, FŎVEO, FŬGIO, become MĀNEO, SĒDEO, FŌVEO, FŪGIO; but FRĪGEO becomes FRĬGEO.

No one, it is presumed, who is familiar with the English method of pronouncing, will deny the justness of this representation of the rules and practice of the English system. But to remove every possible doubt on this point, let us hear Mr. Walker himself, whose rules for pronouncing Greek and Latin proper names have been generally adopted in this country and in England, and whom we cheerfully concede to be the highest authority for the mispronunciation of Greek and Latin words the world has yet produced.

"Every accented antepenultimate but U, even when followed by one consonant only, is, in our pronunciation of Latin as well as of English, short; thus FĀBULA, SĒPARO, DĪLIGO, NŌBILIS, CŬCUMIS, have the first syllables pronounced as in the English words, *capital*, *celebrate*, *simony*, *solitude*, *luculent*, in direct opposition to the Latin quantity, which makes every antepenultimate vowel in all these words but the last, long; and this we pronounce long, though short in Latin. But if a semi-consonant diphthong succeed, then every such vowel is sounded long but I in our pronunciation of both languages; and EUGĂNEUS, EUGĔNIA, FĪLIUS, FŎLIUM, DŬBIA, have the vowel in the antepenultimate syllable pronounced exactly as in the English words *satiate*, *menial*, *delirious*, *notorious*, *penurious;* though they are all short in Latin but the I, which we pronounce short, though in the Latin it is long."

In all these accented antepenults, then, Mr. Walker *expressly* requires every long vowel to be shortened and every short vowel to be lengthened.

As another illustration of the inherent and insuperable difficulties under which the English system labors in respect to the giving of Latin quantity, take the verb FUGIO in its four principal parts; FŬGIO, FŬGERE, FŪGI, FŬGITUM. If now the attempt be made to distinguish the long and short sounds of the U, pronouncing the former as in *tube*, and the latter as in *tub*, then according as the G is made hard or soft, we shall have either FŬG-Ĭ-O, FŬG-Ĕ-RE, FŪ-JI, FŬG-Ĭ-TUM, or FŬDG-I-O, FŬDG-E-RE, FŪ-JI, FŬDG-I-TUM. But this is a little too *fudg-y* even for our English pronouncer, and so, in perfect consistency with himself and his intelligent guides, he concludes to violate the quantity in three cases out of the four.

The proper quantity of final syllables and monosyllables is rarely given. The latter are generally pronounced short except where they *are* short, *e. g.*, ōs, *the mouth*, is made short. Nīl, coming by syncopation and contraction from NĬHĬL, is made short, but the short first vowel of the full form is changed into a diphthong, *naihil;* thus the word, at one time, is robbed of half its quantity, and, at another, has one half more than its due. On the other hand, QVĔ, VĔ, NĔ, TĔ, etc., are made long. Es, however, whether it be a final syllable or a monosyllable, is always long, whatever its real quantity.

Again, this system of capriciously changing both the quantities and the sounds of the vowels according to their position, becomes most ludicrously conspicuous in the inflectional variations of words. In the declensions of nouns, the radical vowel, which has and should receive the same quantity and sound throughout, is changed from short to long or long to short and back again with startling rapidity and frequency, the sound also varying with the quantity. Ōs, *the mouth*, goes thus: ŏs, ŌRĬS, ŌRĪ, ŏs, ŏs, ŌRĒ, etc.; MĪLĔS, goes thus: MĪLĒS, MĬLĬTĬS, MĬLĬTĪ, MĬLĬTĔM, MĪLĒS, MĬLĬTĒ, etc.: the plural of MITIS, *mild*, goes thus: MĪTĒS, MĪTĒS, MĬTĬA; MĬTĬŬM, MĬTĬŬM, MĬTĬŬM; MĬTĬBŬS, MĬTĬBŬS, MĬTĬBŬS; MĪTĒS, MĪTĒS, MĬTĬĂ, etc., pronounced MA̅I̅-TĒZ, MA̅I̅-TĒZ, MĬSH-Y̌-A; MĬSH-Y̌-UM, MĬSH-Y̌-UM, MĬSH-Y̌-UM; MĬT-Y̌-BŬS, MĬT-Y̌-BŬS, MĬT-Y̌-BŬS; MA̅I̅-TĒZ, MA̅I̅-TĒZ, MĬSH-Y̌-A, etc. So also in the variations of verbs. Where the quantity and sound of the radical vowel are really unchanged, they are constantly changing in our pronunciation; and on the other hand, where the quantity is actually changed, distinguishing contracted and uncontracted forms or indicating difference of tense or action, we neglect the distinction, and make the different quantities alike long or alike short. Sometimes we even reverse the facts, making the short long, and the long short, Thus in the imperfect tenses, LĔGO, LĔGEBAM, the short E of the present is made long; and in the perfect tenses, LĒGI, LĒGERAM, the long E of the pluperfect is made short. We make no distinction between the E of PĒS and that of PĔDIS. In BŌS, BŎVIS, the O of the nominative, which has become long by contraction, is made short, while the short O of the genitive is made long. In VĔNIO, VĔNIRE, VĒNI, etc., we make no distinction between the short E of the present and the long E of the perfect. And still further; as, on the one hand, we lengthen the short E in most of the imperfect tenses, so, on the other, we shorten the long E in all the perfect tenses except the dissyllabic VENI.

Such are some of the many ways in which the English system of Latin pronunciation necessarily violates the true quantities of the language, and is, therefore, fatal to the proper rhythm of Latin verse. These multitudinous and glaring corruptions, which, against many earnest protests, gradually invaded and finally supplanted the older and purer English method of pronouncing Latin, are now, as we have seen, systematically inculcated in our Latin grammars and other elementary works. But no ingenuity of man can harmonize the parts of this system. The rules laid down for the sounds of the letters are often, and of necessity, in direct conflict with those given by the same authority for the quantity of syllables, so that, if the pupil gives the prescribed *sound* he will violate the *quantity*, or if he gives the *quantity*, he will violate the rule for the *sound*. Numerous illustrations of this fact might be drawn from the Latin grammars most commonly used in our schools and colleges. One or two will be sufficient for our purpose.

"I is long in the first syllable of a word, the second of which is accented: 1st. When it stands alone before a consonant. 2d. When it ends a syllable before a vowel."

The example adduced in illustration of the first part of this rule is ĬDONEUS, in which the initial I is *short*. With the second, viz., I *is long when it ends a syllable before a vowel*, compare the first general rule of quantity, "A vowel before another vowel is *short*."

Again, "When a syllable ends with a consonant, it has always the *short* English sound."

The student who reads this brief and comprehensive rule, and understands the meaning of words, must consider the whole question for ever settled with regard to the quantity of a syllable ending in a consonant. But what is his surprise when, in the chapter on Quantity, he observes a long succession of rules with numerous exceptions on this very subject of the quantity of syllables ending in a consonant. And his wonder and perplexity are still further increased when he reads the following rule of quantity: "A vowel naturally short before two consonants is *long*."

Now what is the actual effect of this corrupted system of pronunciation upon the English and American method of reading Latin verse? It is obvious that the real quantity, as indicated and determined by the sounds, is entirely disregarded. The line is simply divided into the proper number of feet, and the foot into the proper number of syllables. These syllables are assumed to be long or short, according to the exigencies of the case, though they may be *sounded* of the opposite quantity, and then the rhythm is secured by giving the ICTUS to the proper syllable of the foot. This system of scanning, then, though professedly resting on quantity, is really, like the English, based on accentuation. For example, take the 10th and 11th lines of the first book of the Æneid:

ĪNSĪG|NĒM PĬĔ|TĀTĔ VĬ|RŪM, TŎT Ă|DĪRĔ LĂ|BŌRĒS,
ĪMPŬLĔ|RĪT. TĀN|TA̅E̅NE ĂNĬ|MĪS CO̅E̅|LĒSTĬBŬS|ĪRA̅E̅?

In the first foot of the first line, the two long syllables are pronounced short; in the second, the long is made short and the two shorts, long; in the third, the two shorts are made long, the short I in VIRUM as well as in PIETATE, being also changed to a diphthong; in the fourth, the long is made short; in the fifth, the two shorts are made long: in the first foot of the second, the long is made short, and the two shorts, long; in the second, the two longs are made short; in the fourth, the first long is made short; in the fifth, the long is made short. In the first eleven lines this English method requires the violation of Latin quantity, as indicated by its own rules and sounds, about seventy times. The rhythm is made to depend solely upon raising the voice in the ARSIS, and lowering it in the THESIS of the foot. Closely connected with this, and a natural consequence of it, is the almost universal and yet utterly abominable practice of separating the *feet* instead of the *words* by slight CAESURAS. Each word does not stand by itself as it should, and as it does in prose, but the syllables which constitute the foot, though forming parts of different words, stand by themselves. Whenever, therefore, the foot ends in the middle of a word, as it frequently will in all melodious verse, the parts of the word are improperly separated by a CAESURA.

I claim now to have fully substantiated the charges brought against the present English system of Latin pronunciation, and shown it to be liable to very grave objections. We have also seen that the so-called "Continental" method is entitled neither to the authority implied in that name, nor to any respect based on grounds of intrinsic worth; and we may safely take it for granted that the scholars of England and America will not servilely copy the usage of any single nation on the Continent, as France or Germany, Italy or Spain. Finally, we have found the original Roman system of pronunciation fully developed by the researches of the learned, and established by complete and satisfactory evidence. And the question naturally arises, can this system, in theory so beautiful and so authentic, be revived in practice? This question has sometimes been answered negatively by persons who maintain that the man who has, in substance, the true theory of the Romans in pronouncing their language, and attempts to carry it out in his own pronunciation of the Latin, may, in many instances, depart from the actual practice of the Romans. Possibly he may; it is hardly possible, we know, for a living language to maintain its original form in all respects unchanged through successive centuries. But yet, in view of the exceeding simplicity and symmetry of the Roman system, he has, I think, a better reason to suppose that he *does not*, than anybody else has to suppose that he *does*. And besides, whether in the application of the theory, he does or does not vary, occasionally, from the actual usage of the Romans, is a question nearly as immaterial as it is manifestly undebatable. Of course, no man can know or reasonably pretend to know, whether his pronunciation of the Latin corresponds *precisely* with that of Cicero or Cæsar, but with the well authenticated and simple theory of the Romans before him, he may be reasonably assured that his pronunciation is substantially identical with theirs. He may not, for instance, be sure whether he gives to F the same degree of aspiration that the Romans did; whether he sounds the V consonant, or the rare and difficult combinations EI and EU, precisely as they did; but he may be certain that he sounds all the vowels and all the common diphthongs as they did; that he makes the same consonants *gutturals*, *linguals* or *labials*; *mutes*, *liquids* or *spirants*; the same mutes, *soft*, *hard* or *rough* which the

Romans did; he may thus know that he has the full *idea* on which the entire Roman system was based, and may be reasonably assured that his actual practice is substantially identical with the Roman.

But, admitting the possibility of restoring the true pronunciation, can not all the advantages of its restoration be secured without the inconvenience and singularity of a change? Why not, it has sometimes been asked, teach the Roman pronunciation in *theory* for purposes of comparative philology, but follow the English system in *practice*, to avoid being singular? In this position we have, I think, two unwarrantable assumptions. 1st, that a mere theoretical knowledge of the Roman pronunciation is all we need for the successful study of the relations of the Latin to its sister languages, and 2d, that the study of Comparative Philology is the only thing to be promoted by our knowledge of Roman orthoëpy. Admitting, for the moment, the truth of the second assumption, viz.: that Comparative Philology is the only thing to be affected by our knowledge or ignorance of Roman orthoëpy —is it true, we ask, that a merely theoretical knowledge of the Roman pronunciation is amply sufficient for all purposes of comparative philology?

It would seem to me that the mere statement of this question is amply sufficient for the refutation ot this assumption. The mere knowledge of the Roman *theory* of pronunciation without the habitual *practice* of that pronunciation is, to my mind and in my experience, of *comparatively* little utility in respect to the study of the foreign affinities of the Latin language. I maintain that the Roman pronunciation becomes valuable to the student of the character and relations of the Latin just in proportion to his *familiarity* with it. It is the constant speaking, and reading, and study of the language, on the Roman system of orthoëpy—it is this accustoming of the *ear* to the Roman sounds, and this *alone*, I had almost said, which sheds a continuous and ever increasing light on its foreign relations; and opens successively new and attractive vistas into the wide field of comparative philology. It must be so from the nature of the case. The affinities between the words of sister languages lie especially in their *radical sounds*, *i. e.*, in the sounds of their root-letters. While these sounds may be substantially identical—sounds which the sister nations had in common long before they had a written language, and even when they were yet, in fact, but one nation—the alphabetical representations of those sounds adopted by the separated members of the one original family after the time of their separation, may be, and in fact are, widely diverse. How different, for example, the *appearance* of the Saxon *tomb* and the Latin TUMULUS; of the Saxon *kink* and the Latin CINCTUM; and how different their *sounds*, also, on the English method of pronouncing Latin. But, on the Roman method, the two Saxon words have, respectively, the precise sounds of the *roots* of the two Latin words, TUM-ulus and CINC-tum. Now which of the two, I ask, will the more readily discover this affinity, the man who, though informed of the Roman theory, *practices* the English; who *habitually* gives to those Latin words their foreign, false, unrelated sounds, or, the man to whose ear the true Roman and related sounds are perfectly familiar? The question needs no formal answer. To study with advantage, then, the relations of the Latin to other languages, the real *sounds* of the language must be familiar to the *ear;* and they never can become so except by their being familiar on the *tongue.*

But is there any truth in the second of the above assumptions, viz., that comparative philology is the only thing to be affected by our knowledge or ignorance of Roman orthoëpy? Very far from it. An auricular familiarity with the Roman system of pronunciation, I deem to be quite as valuable an aid in the study of the language itself, as in that of comparative philology, and, therefore, of far greater practical value, inasmuch as few persons will have leisure to carry their investigations into the field of Comparative Philology, while thousands are engaged in the study of the Latin, and interested in having their knowledge of that language as accurate and complete as the researches of the learned can make it. If I may be allowed to refer to my own experience, I would say that I am fully conscious of having made more real progress in the study of the language itself, as well as of its affinities, during the first five years in which I practiced the Roman pronunciation, than I did by the harder study of the preceding ten years in the use of the English system ; although then not ignorant of the principal points of difference between the Roman and English methods of pronouncing Latin. And from the very nature of things it could not be otherwise. In the study of every language, it is a matter of vast importance to have the right pronunciation, the *true vocal sounds* of the language, not merely in the head, but habitually and familiarly on the tongue. Truth here, as everywhere, is, in itself, an argument sufficient to outweigh a mountain of objections. Nor do I see how a professed *teacher of Latin* can answer it to his conscience or sense of honor, deliberately and elaborately to train his pupils in a way which, by his own confession, misrepresents the form of the language and will as certainly belie its spirit. For the true vernacular pronunciation of a language is necessarily homogeneous with its structure—it is part and parcel of the *genius* of the language. Having been developed and established simultaneously with the growth and maturity of the language itself, they must, of necessity, be so thoroughly harmonized and adjusted to each other, that they can not be severed without great practical disadvantage and loss. I think it may be laid down as a universal truth, that no student of any language can possibly, by any ingenuity, discover and comprehend the real structure and genius of the language as fully and clearly on a foreign and false, as on the true, vernacular system of orthoëpy. I am persuaded from the experience of twenty-four years in teaching Latin, seventeen on the English and seven on the Roman system, that I can teach the important principles of the language far more successfully with the true than with the false pronunciation. I have given the two systems a fair trial with no interest but to ascertain the truth; and I not merely *think* but I *know* that, by the daily use of the true pronunciation, I can secure, on the part of the student, a much more intelligent and lively interest in questions pertaining to the etymology of the language; to its various inflectional forms and laws; to its quantities; and, above all, to its metrical system and its relations to kindred languages. The only and the all-satisfactory explanation of these facts is simply this, that over all the important questions connected with the structure and ethnical relations of the Latin language, the English method of pronouncing it, so far as it differs from the Roman, spreads a cloud which the student must himself clear away, or with difficulty penetrate, in order to any considerable success in his studies, while on these same questions the Roman pronunciation throws a strong light. The false pronunciation necessarily darkens and obstructs the student's pathway; the true one illuminates and clears it. The man who, in the use of the former, has achieved much in Latin philology, would have achieved much more in the use of the latter. What he has accomplished has been done in despite of adverse influences. He has been rowing his Latin boat ADVERSO FLUMINE instead of FLUMINE SECUNDO.

As a preparation for a proper observance of Latin quantity and metre, the position which I am controverting, viz., teach the Roman system of pronunciation, but practice the English, is just about as rational as it would be to expect that, by teaching a child the theory of virtue while you habituate him to the practice of vice, he will ultimately become a virtuous man. It is not mere theoretical principles, but well established moral habits which control the life. The wise man does not say, "*Teach* the child" (theoretically) "the way he should go and when he is old," etc., but "*train up* the child." *Form him to right habits.* The same general principle is involved in this matter of Latin quantity and measure. Accustom your pupil to the English system of pronunciation and, no matter what you teach him, you are *forming him to wrong habits.* You are "training him up" in the way he should *not* go, through the noble measures of Horace and Virgil, Ovid and Juvenal. On this point, I shall have a word or two more to say by-and-by. But of this one thing let every teacher of English-Latin be assured. He can not continue to impose upon his pupils a system of pronunciation so entirely incongruous with that which belongs to the language, and is really and essentially part of itself, and save them from the confusion and error which that system necessarily involves. We may, if we choose, through indolence or timidity, refuse to abandon the worse for the better method; but let us do it with our eyes open. Let us make up our minds clearly on the only alternative that is before us, either to forego the advantages attending on the truth or frankly to abandon and boldly to repudiate the falsehood.

The most important reasons for adopting the latter branch of this alternative have already been foreshadowed in the preceding pages, and some of them have been so fully developed as, perhaps, to need no further illustration. I shall content myself, therefore, in conclusion, with a recapitulation of the main points of the argument, with such expansion and such additional considerations as may seem requisite.

I advocate, then, the adoption of the system of Latin pronunciation above described, in lieu of every other system, and especially of the English:

1. Because it is the true *Roman* pronunciation, and, therefore, in full harmony with the entire structure and genius of the language. This fact

alone is, in my judgment, a sufficient reason for the course proposed.

2. Because it is more simple, regular and philosophical than the English system. Each alphabetical character represents but one articulate sound; and these sounds, whether vowel or consonant, are easily classified or combined in accordance with clear, definite, and invariable phonetic laws.

3. Because it is more euphonious and beautiful than the English system. Let any man of candor and good literary taste go through, for example, with the forms of REGO, REGERE, JUNGO, JUNGERE, first on the Roman plan, giving the E, U, and G their appropriate sounds throughout, and then on the English plan, changing frequently and radically the sounds of the vowels, and also that of the G from a guttural to a lingual spirant and back again; let him decline, on the two plans, AMICUS, ROGUS, the plural of MITIS, FELIX, etc.; let him pronounce, on the two plans, such words as JUSTITIA, AUDACIA, CILICIA, GALATIA, INIMICITIA, INSCITIA, OCEANUS, OFFICIUM, ROSACEUM, OTIUM, NEGOTIUM, INITIUM, etc., etc.; let him, I say, in these and hundreds of other like cases, carefully compare the two systems in respect of their euphony, and *then* defend the English system if he can. It is not uncommon for

persons who have been accustomed only to the English sounds, and whose classical scholarship is not sufficient to enable them to appreciate the intrinsic merits and defects of the two systems, to attempt to cast ridicule upon the strange words revealed by the Roman pronunciation; such, *e. g.*, as those in which C and G occur before E, I, Y, AE, and OE. Ridicule is the most available weapon in a weak cause. But as well might a rude Thracian have laughed at the polished discourse of the sage of the Athenian Academy; as well might a driveling, reeling inebriate, meeting a sober and upright man and fancying him to be the stammering staggerer, sneer at his really clear speech and steady gait, as an English-Latinist cast ridicule upon the pronunciation of a Roman-Latinist. The Roman system of Latin pronunciation must be pronounced, by every competent judge, to be intrinsically far more euphonious and dignified than the English.

4. Because it *always* distinguishes words of different orthography and signification by their *sounds*, while the English system *very frequently* does not; as, *e. g.*, CENSEO, CENSIO, SENTIO; CENSUS and SENSUS; CERVUS and SERVUS; CAEDO, CEDO and SEDO; CICER and SISER; CEU and SEU; CELLA and SELLA; CITUS and SITUS; SCIS and SIS; SCIN (for

SCISNE) and SIN; AMICI and AMISI; CIRCŬLUS and SURCŬLUS; etc., etc. Now when we make such radical changes as these, it is not a mere change in the pronunciation of a word but an actual substitution of one word for another. When we say that SENSUS means *a valuation* (CENSUS) we state a falsehood; SERVUS signifies not *a stag* (CERVUS) but *a slave;* SELLA, not *a room* (CELLA) but *a chair;* SEDO, not *I smite* (CAEDO), nor *I yield* (CEDO) but *I soothe;* etc., etc.

5. Because it diffuses universal light while the English system spreads more or less darkness over the etymology of the language, and over the entire subject of vowel, diphthongal and consonant combinations and changes. This point has already perhaps been sufficiently illustrated. I will only say here that the instances, in which the one system illuminates and the other obscures questions respecting the derivation, composition or orthographical variation of words, occur on every page of every Roman author.

6. Because it not merely throws much light on the subject of Latin versification, but is the only system on which Latin poetry can be correctly read. That this statement is true in regard to Latin quantity has already been shown. It is also

true in two or three other respects. Whenever, for example, the letter c is left at the end of a word, after a final vowel or final M with a preceding vowel has been cut off before a word commencing with a vowel, the c, on the English system of pronunciation, is often improperly transferred from its own to the following word, or changes its sound from K to S or S to K; but on the Roman system, the c always remains with its own word, and its power is unchanged.

So again, QV, when similarly left at the end of a word, must, on the English system, be connected in syllabication with the following word. And thus the QV of one word unite with the first syllable of the next to form either another word or what is no word at all. Every man who reads Latin poetry with the English pronunciation *always* commits this barbarism. He can not do otherwise. Because the sounds of KW represented by QV on the English system, can not be uttered at the end of a syllable, and must, therefore, in all such cases, be severed from their own word and connected with the following. Take, *e. g.*, the following dactylic hexameter from Juvenal:

"SED QVAMQVAM IN MAGNIS OPIBUS PLUMAQVE PATERNA."

The final M of the conjunction with the vowel

preceding are cut off, and on the English system we must read

SED| QVAM|| QV' IN| MAG||NIS, etc.

The *hearer* would, of course, take the second word to be QVAM (*kwam*) and the third, QVIN (*kwin.*) But, on the Roman system, the QVAMQV' sounds like KAMK; the final QV, then, is sounded with its own word; the preposition IN stands properly by itself; and the Roman hearer would know at once from the sound KAMK that the word was QVAMQVAM with the AM cut off by ecthlipsis. Take again Virgil's

"MULTA QVOQVE ET BELLO PASSUS, DUM CONDERET URBEM."

On the English system, we necessarily divide as follows, viz.:

MŪL|TĂ| QVŎ||QV' ĔT| BĔL||LŌ| PĀS||SŪS, etc.

In this reading, the third word QVET (*kwet*) is just no word at all. But on the Roman system, we divide thus:

MŪL|TĂ| QVŎQV|| ĔT| BĔL||LŌ| PĀS||SŪS, etc.
(KŎK)

Here again each word stands properly by itself, and the hearer knows that the second and third words are not KWO and KWET, but QVOQVE (KŎKE) and ET. The QVŎQV' remains short because the QV never form position.

So, a few lines below, we read, on the English system:

. . . . STŬ|DĬ||ĪS| QV' ĀS||PĒR|RĬ|MĂ|| BĒL|LĪ;

but on the Roman system,

. . . . STŬ|DĬ||ĪSQV'| Ā||SPĒR|RĬ|MĂ|| BĒL|LĪ.||
(STŬ|DĬ||ĪSK)

So again, in Horace, we read the following lines on the Roman system, thus:

NŌN| Ĕ|GĒT| MĀU||RĪS| JĂ|CŬ|LĪS|| NĔQV'| ĀR|CŪ;||·
(NĔK)

but on the English system,

NŌN| Ĕ|GĒT| MĀU||RĪS| JĂC|Ŭ|LĪS|| NĔ|QV'ĀR|CŪ.

If there were any truth in spirit rapping, no man, in reading this passage, would utter that word QVARCU or NEQVARCU (*nekwarcu*), without getting, *instanter*, a terrible rap from the spirit of my friend Horace; but as there is not, I feel myself in duty bound to do a little *honest* rapping for him. The instances in which QV is thus left at the end of a word by the cutting off of a final vowel or final AM, EM, IM, OM, or UM, before a word commencing with a vowel, are innumerable, and on the English system, therefore, we are forced, in the reading of Latin poetry, to the perpetration of innumerable barbarisms.

7. Because it facilitates immensely the study of comparative philology, especially when prosecuted with a view to the illustration of the Latin language.

In tracing the affinities among different languages, we must examine especially the *roots* of words, and these roots in respect of their elementary *sounds*, not of their different modes of alphabetical representation; and in order to pursue this path of inquiry with safety and success, we must know accurately and familiarly the affinities of articulate sounds and their natural and legitimate changes and interchanges. The habit of judging of words by the *eye* rather than the *ear*—a habit engendered among cultivated nations by the use of a written language—greatly obstructs that quick perception of the affinities of sounds which has been observed to exist in rude, unlettered tribes. This habit of comparing words by their outward appearance, and not by the sounds of their radical elements, often becomes so strong and fixed that the substitution of one character for another of the same class or organ, a mere vowel change, or a transposition of the root-letters, is sufficient to hide from our view the most perfect affinities. And further, the obscurity and confusion in which the irregularity of the English alphabet tends to involve all our ideas respecting the nature and relations of articulate sounds—an irregularity which, on the one hand, frequently either assigns to one and the same character elementary sounds uttered by different organs or with different degrees of articulation, or, on the other, employs a variety of characters to represent one and the same sound—present to the English and American student still greater obstacles to the successful study of comparative philology. The only remedy for both these evils—the obtuseness of our perception of affinities and the vagueness and confusion of our ideas of affinity—is to teach the English alphabet in such a way as to give an early and familiar acquaintance with the nature and legitimate mutations of articulate sounds; and the true Roman system of notation furnishes the best possible basis on which to impart this instruction and effect this remedy. If we were taught, from our first entrance upon the study of Latin, to classify the letters, especially the consonants, according to their different organs of utterance or degrees of articulation, and were uniformly accustomed to a close observation of the relations of letters and to the examination and comparison of words by their radical sounds and not by their mere outward forms, these interchanges of sounds of the same class, so frequent in different dialects of the same language and different languages of the same family would no longer escape or surprise us. We should then readily discover, where we should otherwise naturally overlook, such affinities as the following, *e. g.*, Latin GeLiDus, German KaLT, English CoLD; Greek ΒΡέΜω, Latin FReMo; Greek 'ΡίΓος, Latin FRiGus; Greek ΡηΓνυμι, Latin FRanGo (root FRaG), English, BReaK; Latin ViGilo, German WaCHen, English WaKe, WatCH; Latin DoCeo, Anglo-Saxon TaeCan, English, TeaCH;* Latin NOX (root, NoCT), German NaCHT, English NiGHT; Latin TRaho, English DRaw, DRag; German DuRST, English THiRST; Latin PaNDo, English BeND; Latin GeRo, English CaRry; Latin FeRo, English BeaR; etc., etc

Now it is obvious that a very large proportion of the affinities existing between the Latin and the other members of the Indo-European family of languages are discoverable only on the Roman system of pronunciation, since the affinities themselves exist only between the Roman sounds of the root-letters and the radical sounds of the corresponding

* The Anglo Saxon c has here, as elsewhere, suffered the same corruption in English which the Roman c has in Italian.

words in the cognate tongues. It follows, therefore, that, in the study of the foreign relations of the Latin language and of comparative philology in general, the man to whose ears the Roman pronunciation is entirely familiar, has immensely the advantage of him who is unfamiliar with it. And such familiarity will be acquired, on the part of the English or American student, only by the constant practice of the Roman system.

Instances in illustration of the affinities between Latin words, and words of similar sound and import in the kindred languages—affinities which are apparent on the Roman pronunciation, but obscured by the English—might be adduced almost AD INFINITUM. Take, *e. g.*, the following Latin and Greek words: ACĔSIS and *ἄκεσις*, a kind of borax; ACOETIS and *ἄκοιτις*, a concubine; ACIES and *ἄκις*, *ἄκη*, a point or edge of any thing; CEDRUS and *κέδρος*, a cedar tree; CEDRIS and *κέδρις*, the fruit of the cedar; CELAENAE and Κελαιναι; CELLO (from which ANTECELLO, etc.) and *κέλλω*, to move, put in quick motion; akin to which are, CELER, quick; CELES, a race-horse; CELOX, a fast-sailing yacht, and *κέλης*, quick, and also (sc. *ἵππος*) a race-horse, and (sc. *ναῦς*) a little boat, pinnace or yacht; CERA and *κηρὸς*, wax; CENTRUM and *κεντρον*; CErăsus and κέρᾰσος, a cherry-tree; cercūrus and κέρκουρος, a light sailing-vessel; cibōrium and κιβώριον, a drinking-cup; cīci and κίκι, the castor-oil plant; cīcĭnus and κίκῖνος; circaeum and κιρκᾶιον, a mandrake; cista and κίστη, a box or chest; cithara and κιθάρα; Cirrha and Κίῤῥα; Circe and Κίρκη; Circaeus and Κιρκᾶιος, of or belonging to Circe; circĭnus and κίρκινος, a pair of compasses; cete and κητη, a whale; coelum and κὄιλος (English, *hollow*); Cinyps and Κίνυψ; Cineas and Κινέας; Celtae and Κέλται; Cilicia and Κιλικία; cinaedus and κίναιδος, an unchaste person; Cittĭum and Κίττιον; gemo and γεμω, to groan; genĕsis and γένεσις; gerrae and γεῤῥα; Getae and Γέται; gypsum and γύψος; gyrus and γῦρος; Gythium and Γύθιον; scilla, or sqvilla, and σκίλλα, a sea-onion; sciūrus and σκίουρος, a squirrel; qve and καὶ; cestus and κεστὸς, a girdle; census and κῆνσος, a tax; cincinnus and κίκιννος, a ringlet of hair; ciccus and κίκκος, the fruit-core; cio and κίω, to move, etc.; circus and κίρκος, etc., etc.: or the following Latin and German, or Greek words: ag-er and *ack-er*, a field; aqv-a and *ach*, water, as in *Biberach;* cella and *keller*, a room; coqvus or cocus and *koch*, a cook; vacillare and *wackeln*, to waver, totter;

MŪRUS and *mauer;* MŪS and *maus;* SUG-ERE and *saug-en*, to suck; CISTA and *kiste;* CICER and *kicher*, a chick-pea; COENA (*κοῖνος*, common) and *koena*, which, in some parts of Silesia, is the word for the common meal; CARCER, Greek *κάρκαρον*, German *kerker*, Welsh *carcar*, a prison; CAESAR and *Kaiser;* CEVA and *kuh*, English *cow;* NATŪRA and *natúr;* COELUM (*κοῖλον*) and *hohl*, *höhle*, *hollow;* VICIA and *wicke*, a vetch; CERASUS and *kirsche;* JUG-UM and *joch*, a yoke; AC-IES and *eck-e*, a point, corner; ACER (ϝACER) and *wacker*, fierce, valiant; VIGILO and *wack-en;* FAC-IO and *mach-en;* HESTERN-US and *gestern*, etc., etc.: or the following Latin and Saxon, or Welsh words: CINC-TUM and *kink;* TUM-ULUS and *tomb;* PUP-PIS and *poop*, the stern of a ship; CISTA and Welsh *cist;* CROC-IO and *croak;* SCINC-US and *skink*, a kind of lizard; ALC-IS and *elk;* GEN-US and *kin*, *kind*, as a noun; etc., etc.

8. Because it greatly augments the incidental and collateral advantages connected with the study of the Latin language. The value of a thorough knowledge of the Latin to the student of general philology is universally conceded, and can hardly be over-estimated. Constituting, as it does, the basis of all the languages of south-western Europe,

and being, at the same time, in its essential elements, most intimately allied to the Teutonic and Celtic families—so intimately that some distinguished scholars have been disposed to consider it a daughter rather than a sister of the German, and others, to regard it as simply a dialectical development of the Celtic language; and others still, as Reinhold Klotz, have more recently, and with more correctness, considered it to be, in its original and essential elements, Celto-Germanic, but developed under a controlling Grecian spirit and influence—sustaining, I say, these intimate relations to the Celtic, Teutonic, and Romance languages, it forms the connecting link between them; while many of these again, Celtic, Teutonic, Latin, and its daughter, the Norman-French, have each contributed largely to the formation of our own language; so that a correct knowledge of the Latin becomes indispensable to the full understanding of either the English or any of the south-western European tongues. It is obvious, then, that the use of the Roman system of pronunciation—a system which is itself an integral and vital part of the genius of the language, and as such absolutely essential to the full comprehension of its structure and spirit, and which is also closely allied to the vocal systems of the cognate languages — must greatly enhance all the incidental and collateral advantages to be derived from the study of the Latin, and this in two ways; 1st, indirectly, by imparting a far more correct and intimate knowledge of the Latin itself; and, 2d, directly, by preparing the way, especially to the English and American student, whose vernacular orthoëpy is so alien from that of the kindred tongues, for the more ready and thorough acquisition of the languages of modern Europe. Were we to study the Latin on the Roman system of orthoëpy, it would be found that the shortest road to a thorough knowledge of either of the more cultivated continental languages would not only commence with and run through the Latin, but, even after leaving the Latin, would be greatly smoothed and facilitated, to its very termination, by a familiar acquaintance with the true pronunciation of the Latin.

9. Because it is the only system on which a uniform pronunciation can ever be secured even in our own country, to say nothing of uniformity among the different modern civilized nations. In our country there is, at the present time, a great diversity of systems. "A very few," says that accomplished Latin scholar, the late Robert Kelly,

LL.D., in the article above mentioned, "employ the continental vowel sounds, but let the diphthongs and certain consonants suffer. Some give the true sound of the letter A, but give E the sound of I, I the sound of the English *i* in pine, Œ the sound of E, etc. Others are still more barbarian, giving A the sound of E, Æ and Œ the sound of I, with other atrocious aberrations from the true standard. The ears of persons trained in one of these schools are offended with the pronunciation given by the others, and would be offended in like manner if the true pronunciation were given. Indeed, we have heard of instances where the professor has assailed with ridicule pupils who came to him with a *Roman* pronunciation." In immediate connection with this he asks, "Why can we not, with one consent, abandon our erroneous modes of pronouncing Latin, and adopt an uniform and correct pronunciation?" And then, after giving the Roman scheme, he adds: "Now, what can be desired or imagined simpler than this whole scheme? . . . . . . The sounds are all familiar, and can be learned with the utmost facility. The unlearning of the various false methods will not be found a difficult undertaking by any one who will set about it. The most inveterate barbarian, by reading aloud for an hour or two a day, will in a fortnight metamorphose himself into a veritable 'old Roman.' It will probably be more difficult to persuade scholars to adopt the hard sounds of C and G where they now make them soft, than to assent to any other change required. Some words will strike them ludicrously. They will recalcitrate against restoring to the great Roman orator his good name, of which he has been so long and so unreasonably deprived. But there can be nothing intrinsically ridiculous or undignified in the pronunciation which classic antiquity uttered. 'Tis better to give to Scipio and Cicero the names by which they were called when in the flesh, and which they invested with immortal glory—far better all these changes—than, as Kraitzer hath it, 'to turn the pompous senate of Rome into a mass of hissing serpents.' The true pronunciation will, as a matter of course, become to us infinitely more harmonious, dignified and expressive, than the dissonant utterances by which we have so long caricatured the noble language. . . . . . Of what importance is the retention of the false methods that within two centuries have invaded the language? There is nothing about them which entitles them to respect, and every American scholar who visits continental Europe and attempts to speak or read Latin, is perfectly ashamed of his pronunciation. . . . . . The irregularity of pronunciation that prevails, the general want of confidence, and the conviction resting oftentimes, upon the mind of the teacher, of the falseness of the system he practices, have a most unfavorable effect on the whole style of reading Latin, and not unfrequently upon a rigid observance of quantity. The facile and correct reading aloud of the classic writers, is not only a beautiful and rare accomplishment, but exercises an important influence upon the taste and upon the appreciation of nameless graces and beauties of style." . . . "The *philological* bearings of a correct pronunciation involve considerations of paramount importance in connection with this question. The argument from philology will press with irresistible force upon the mind of the scholar who will examine the subject carefully."

These eminently scholar-like views and suggestions I have preferred to quote consecutively, though not all bearing specifically upon the present point, viz., the impossibility of restoring or securing in our country an entire uniformity of Latin pronunciation on any other than the Roman system.

Uniformity on the modern English system we have already lost, and can never regain. The hostility of that system to the structure and genius ot the Latin language, has forced many institutions, both in this country and in England, to at least a partial abandonment of it, *i. e.*, to the substitution, in part or in full, of the German vowel sounds for the English. These institutions will be very unlikely to retrace their steps. The intrinsic excellence of the German, or, which is the same thing, of the Roman vowel system, the facility with which, on that system, the true Latin quantities can be observed, and the impossibility of habitually observing them in the English method, the increasing practical convenience of the German system arising from our growing intercourse with the scholars of the Continent, all will unite to prevent such a return to the English vowel sounds. If these institutions change again, they will be morally certain to advance still further toward ancient Rome.

But can the scholars of this country and of England ever unite on the falsely so-called "Continental" method of pronouncing Latin? It is obviously impossible. This combination of the German vowel sounds with the English diphthongal and consonant sounds, though far better than the English system entire, is, after all, a mongrel system —a hybrid—itself the product of an unnatural, uncongenial union—and can never form the basis of a cordial and permanent union among English and American Latinists. The true Latin scholars of our country, the genuine lovers of Roman literature, can never harmonize on a system which subjects the really euphonious and symmetrical language of the Romans to the countless dissonances, irregularities, and serious practical evils occasioned by the false sounds of the diphthongs AE and OE; of C and G before E, I, Y, AE and OE; of QV, J, S and T. A system liable to such grave, intrinsic objections, and wanting the poor outward support of national prejudice and pride, can never commend itself to general respect and adoption.

Again, we may safely assume, I think, that the scholars of this country and of England will never servilely exchange their own national system for that of any single nation on the Continent. They would recalcitrate more instantaneously and violently against saying with the German, *Tsits-ero*, or with the Italian *Chich-ero*, than with the Roman *Ki-kero* (*Kee-kero*, not *Kick*-ero).

We are, then, shut up either to all the serious disadvantages not only of great error but of great diversity in error, or to the adoption of the true Roman system of Latin pronunciation. There is no other alternative. On this, as on other subjects, there can be no intelligent and permanent harmony of view and practice except on the basis of truth; and where shall that basis be found except in the Roman system of orthoëpy? This, and this alone, forms a purely scientific and philosophical ground of uniformity. We must have either a harmonious union in the truth, or disunion and disharmony in error. The true vernacular pronunciation of the Latin language must ultimately prevail in this country and in England, or we are certainly doomed to endless diversity.

And why should we hesitate in regard to this clear, necessary alternative? We have nothing to lose, but every thing to gain, by the cordial adoption of the truth. Aside from our own personal benefits thereby secured, have we not reason to hope that, if English and American scholars should generally adopt the Roman system of Latin pronunciation, the scholars of the Continent would soon follow the example? Might we not expect, in that case, the prediction of Lipsius to be speedily fulfilled? "AUDEAT ENIM UNA ALIQVA (GENS) ET OMNES AUDIENT." The German and Italian scholars would have but few changes to make; chiefly those pertaining to the diphthongs and to the consonant c. If, then, even in Germany, where the departures from Roman usage are so limited, the practical adoption of the entire Roman system is reckoned by some of their best Latin scholars a great desideratum, how much more, in our country and in England, where those departures are so numerous and wide, and where there is now such a diversity of systems, how much more is the general adoption of the Roman system to be earnestly desired; not simply on the all-sufficient ground of its intrinsic superiority, theoretical and practical, to the English system, but also as the only means of securing uniformity among ourselves; of bringing us into harmony with the main features of the German and Italian systems; and possibly, of bringing them into full harmony with us and the Roman system? "Why," then, in the language of Mr. Kelly, "why can we not, with one consent, abandon our erroneous modes of pronouncing Latin, and adopt a uniform and correct pronunciation?" How glorious a day for the study of this noble language would be that in which a uniform pronunciation should be secured on the true Roman basis! O NOCTES COENAEQVE DEUM! O when, it just occurs to me to ask in passing, when shall we Latin scholars have a system of pronunciation which will enable us, with one accord, to utter those words as Horace uttered them, instead of giving four false quantities in those eight syllables, and mispronouncing every syllable but one, as on the English system we not merely do, but *must* do? That single and singularly fortunate exceptional syllable is the interjectional vowel O, in which, it would seem, the English system has the sound right, simply because it is impossible to get it wrong. In the very next syllable, that vowel receives, as it often does on the English method, the sound of *a* in *what* or *o* in *not*, a sound unknown alike to the Latin, the Italian and the German languages. How long shall we continue to inflict a barbarous violence on the elegant and majestic diction of Cæsar and Cicero? of Virgil and Ovid, Horace and Juvenal? How long shall we continue to say, 'MULTA KWO KWET BELLO?' and 'NON EGET MAURIS JACULIS NEKWARCU?'" etc., etc., etc.

Now all the evils connected with our false methods of pronouncing Latin admit of a ready and an effectual remedy. We have but to adopt the perfectly simple and beautiful system of the Romans in pronouncing their language, to make ourselves familiar with it, "at home" in it; and all these evils will have vanished. Nor shall we long continue in the careful, thoughtful practice of the Roman pronunciation, without finding ourselves much more at home in the language itself than we have been or otherwise could be.

The difficulty of making this change is by no means so great as might be supposed. As already suggested in the quotation from Mr. Kelly, the practice of reading Latin aloud correctly for an hour or two a day, will soon create, even in those long accustomed to a false pronunciation, a thorough distaste for their old method, and an earnest love for the new. The true sounds are so harmonious with each other, and with the entire structure and genius of the language, as to commend themselves at once to our enlightened judgment, our chastened and refined ear, and our cordial good will. As we become familiar with the true system, we shall love and prize it. We shall appreciate, as we have never done before, the real majesty of the Latin language; the true dignity and power of Roman eloquence; the genuine harmonies, and smoothly-flowing numbers of Roman verse.

APPENDIX.

Note A.—Page 23.

"The sounds of the long and short vowels, though *elementarily the same*, were *always* distinguished in length. . . . . The sound of the long vowels was that of the short vowels doubled."—*Scheller's Latin Grammar.*

The author of "Living Latin" (London, 1847) says: "That the Latin vowels have only one sound each, long or short, is clear from Priscian, who, when he would enumerate the varieties of sound which they admit, mentions only those of accent and aspiration, which are merely varieties of its accidents, not of the sound itself."

A.

In nearly all the cultivated European languages, ancient or modern, of Celtic, Teutonic or Slavonic origin, the vowel A has an uniform sound like that of *a* in *father*. Prominent among these languages are the Greek, German, Latin and its modern derivatives, the Italian, French, Spanish and Portuguese, and our own mixed vernacular. The exceptions in the sound of the A are limited to the English and French. The Greek A, to which the Latin A is precisely equivalent in power, Dionysius of Halicarnassus describes as being formed with "the mouth as much opened as possible." Pennington, on *The Pronunciation of Greek*, says (page 28): "It seems clear, from the description of Dionysius, that this letter was pronounced as we sound the *a* in *father*. The modern Greeks so sound it, as do most, if not all, of the other nations of Europe." In full accordance with the description of Dionysius are the statements of the Latin authors, Quintilian, Priscian, Terentianus, Victorinus Afer, and Capella, who speak of the vowel as being uttered RICTU PATULO, HIATU ORIS, etc.

E.

This second Latin vowel is heard, according to Varro, in the bleating of the sheep, which may, perhaps, be well represented by the final syllable of the verb o-BEY. It is, therefore, wholly unlike the English E. Its Italian power, which, in its short and long sounds, corresponds to the *E* and *H* of the Greeks, is uniformly recognized throughout continental Europe.

I.

The vowel I, Victorinus describes as being made with the mouth nearly closed. It was recognized, by both Greeks and Romans, as entirely identical with the Greek *I*, which, as Pennington says (page 36), "was sounded like the *e* in *mete*. The modern Greeks so pronounce it; and here, again, the English, in differing from the modern Greeks, differ from all the nations of Europe." Doctor Webster says, "The English *seat* retains the Roman pronunciation of SIT-US, that is, SEETUS."

O.

The character O was intended to represent the position of the lips in forming the sound. Its short and long sounds correspond entirely to the *O* and Ω of the Greeks, in forming which, Dionysius says, "the mouth is rounded, and the lips disposed in a circle, and the breath strikes upon the extremitiy of the lips." The sound of *o* in *not*, therefore, or *a* in *what*, which is often represented to be like the short sound of the Greek, Latin and German o, is a totally different sound, made in a different part of the voice-passage, and with the lips in a very different position—a sound unknown alike to the Greek, Latin, German, Anglo-Saxon, Italian, Spanish, Portuguese, etc.

U.

The vowel U was uttered, as described by Capella, with the lips not only rounded, but protruded, and was articulated in the lips. Its sound is heard in the lowing of kine. Hence the verb MUGIRE, *to low*, *to bellow*, is derived from the sound made by kine in lowing, and represented by the letters MŪ, *mōō*. This vowel, therefore, has invariably the sound of *oo*, long or short, never that of the English *you*. Hence the Greeks, in transferring Latin proper nouns into their own language, always express the Latin U by their diphthong ΟΥ; and the Romans, on the other hand, in translating Greek proper nouns, always employ their U to represent the Greek diphthong.

NOTE B.—PAGE 28.

"AI syllabam, cujus secundam nunc E literam ponimus, varie per A et I efferebant, qvidam semper ut Graeci; qvidam singulariter, tantum cum in dativum vel genitivum casum incidissent."—QVINTIL., l. i., c. 7.

"Ea qvae nos per AE, antiqvi per AI scriptitaverunt, JULIAI CLAUDIAI. Et nihil obstat, qvominus hoc aut illo modo scribamus in utroqve numero."—VELIUS LONGUS.

"Alpha semper atque Iota, qvem parant Graeci sonum, A et E nobis ministrant: sic nos scribimus." —TERENTIANUS.

"Apud antiqvos I litera pro E scribebatur, ut testantur metaplasmi in qvibus est ejus modi syllabarum deductio, ut PICTAI VESTIS, et AULAI IN MEDIO, pro PICTAE et AULAE."—SCAURUS.

NOTE C.—PAGE 31.

"Transit qvoqve AU in O productam more antiqvo, ut LŌTUS pro LAUTUS, PLŌSTRUM pro PLAUS-

TRUM, CŌTES pro CAUTES; sicut etiam contra pro O, AU; ut AUSTRUM pro OSTRUM, AUSCULUM pro OSCULUM; frequentissime hoc faciebant antiqvi."—PRISCIAN.

NOTE D.—PAGE 31.

"AB OLOES antiqvi dicebant pro AB ILLIS."—FESTUS.

"MOERORUM antiqvi pro MŪRORUM; nam veteres pleraqve, eorum qvae nos per U dicimus, per OE diphthongon pronunciabant; et contra PŪNIO pro POENIO, qvod verbum a POENA venit. Hinc est PŪNICA REGNA VIDES, cum POENOS ubiqve legerimus." —SERVIUS.

NOTE E.—PAGE 42.

"Prisci pro ACIPENSER dicebant AQVIPENSER, pro SEXDECIM, SEXDEQVIM. Ex *κάρκερα* fecerunt febrim qverqveram et carcerem, qvia scilicet *κάρκερ* efferebant."—FESTUS.

"Cum Romani, euntes per Tusciam, interrogarent Agyllinos qvae diceretur civitas, illi, ut pote Graeci, qvid audirent ignorantes, et optimum ducentes si eos prius salutarent, dixerunt *χαῖρε*; qvam salutationem Romani nomen civitatis esse putaverunt et, detracta aspiratione, eam CAERE nominaverunt."—JULIUS HYGINUS apud SERVIUM.

NOTE F.—PAGE 42.

"Antiqvi per C literae formam nihilominus G usurpabant. ACETARE dicebant pro AGITARE; PRODIGIA qvod PRODICANT futura, permutatione G literae; nam qvae nunc G appellatur, ab antiqvis C vocabatur, QVINCENTUM per C literam usurpabant antiqvi."—FESTUS.

"Pro agro GABINO dicebant CABINO; pro LEGE, LECE; ACNA pro AGNA. AUCTIO certe ab AUGENDA dicta est; et numeri cum C habeant, ut DUCENTI, SEXCENTI, G reliqvi habent ut QVADRINGENTI, NONGENTI."—VICTORINUS.

"CAMELUM alii dicunt, alii, GAMELUM. NEGOTIUM dictum est qvia NEC OTIUM."—SCAURUS.

NOTE G.—PAGE 45.

"Cum is candidatus, qvi coqvi filius habebatur, coram Cicerone suffragium ab alio peteret, EGO QVOQVE, Cicero inqvit, TIBI JURE FAVEBO, pro EGO COQVE."—QVINCT.

"Ciceronis dictum refertur in eum, qvi coqvi filius secum causas agebat. TU QVOQVE ADERAS HUIC CAUSAE; nam veteres COQVUS non per C literam, sed per Q scribebant."—DONATUS.

"COCUM nonnulli in utraqve syllaba per Q scribunt, nonnulli et inserta V. In verbo enim COQVERE, pro QVOQVERE, NISUS censet ubiqve C literam ponendam, tam in nomine qvam in verbo."—VELIUS LONGUS.

"Apud antiqvos freqventissime loco CU syllabae QVU ponebatur, et e contrario; ut ARQVUS, COQVUS, OQVULUS, QVUM, QVUR."—PRISCIAN.

"QVOTIDIE sunt qvi per co, COTIDIE scribant, qvibus peccare licet desinerent, si scirent inde tractum esse a QVOT DIEBUS, hoc est, OMNIBUS DIEBUS." —ANNAEUS CORNUTUS.

"RELIQVIAE et RELIQVI per C scribebantur, COTIDIE per C et O dicitur et scribitur, pro Q; qvia non QVOTIDIE, sed a CONTINENTE DIE dictum est." —PAPYRIANUS.

"Licinius Calvus Q litera non est usus. Antiqvi CUM adverbium scribebant qvatuor literis QVUM, sed pronunciabant tamen PERINDE AC SI CUM scriptum esset."—VICTORINUS.

NOTE H.—PAGE 46.

"Antiqvi in connexione syllabarum ibi tantum K utebantur ubi A litera subjungenda erat; qvoniam multis vocalibus instantibus, qvoties id verbum scribendum erat, in qvo retinere hae literae nomen suum possent, singulae pro syllaba scribebantur, tanqvam satis eam ipso nomine explerent, ut puta DECIMUS, D per se, inde CIMUS; item CERA, C simplex et RA, et BENE, BEN. Ita et qvoties KANUS, KARUS scribendum erat, qvia singulis literis primae syllabae notabantur, K prima ponebatur, qvae suo nomine A continebat; qvia si C posuissent, CENUS et CERUS futurum erat, non CANUS, et CARUS."—SCAURUS. Cf. also ARISTARCHUS, De Arte Gram., lib. i., cap. xvii.

NOTE I.—PAGE 40.

"Et nostrarum ultima X, qva tamen carere potuimus, si non qvaesissemus."—QUINT., i., iv.

"Latini voces qvae in X literam incidunt, si in declinatione earam apparebat G, scribebant GS, ut CONJUGS, LEGS."—VICTORINUS.

"X duplicem loco C et S, vel G et S postea a Graecis inventam, assumpsimus, ut DUX, DUCIS; REX, REGIS."—PRISCIAN.

"Ante Augustum CS vice X."—ISIDORUS.

www.ingramcontent.com/pod-product-compliance
Lightning Source LLC
LaVergne TN
LVHW021425110826
845150LV00007B/2094